PAR 10,000

# PAR 10,000

## A GOLFING ODYSSEY ACROSS MOUNTAINS, MOORS AND FIELDS

## DAVID EWEN

MAINSTREAM
PUBLISHING

EDINBURGH AND LONDON

First published in Great Britain in 2001 by
MAINSTREAM PUBLISHING COMPANY (EDINBURGH) LTD
7 Albany Street
Edinburgh EH1 3UG

ISBN 1 84018 444 2

A catalogue record for this book is available from the British Library

Typeset in Berkeley, City and Univers
Printed and bound in Great Britain by Creative Print and Design Wales

# HOLES

# Foreword

IT WAS THE most satisfying golf shot I have ever hit. There was no flag to aim at, no bunker or rough to clear, no bevelled green to surmount, no objective measure of my performance. Just rows of houses, some parked cars and a big hedge at the end of the street. I was in my front garden. There's a photograph of the occasion: me leaning on the driver like it was a crook, a boy wielding a man's tool.

At ten years old you don't need a sports psychologist to tell you to see only the target, not the obstacles. You don't even need a target. To unleash the ball is enough, to watch it taking off and flying under your own nascent power. A golf club is a machine after all, a multiplier of force, but back then it might have been a magic wand.

All this thrilled – and also the possibility that this white blob would take out windows, dent cars and poleaxe anyone who got in its way.

I could have played safe, chosen a putter and trundled the ball from one end of the lawn to the other. I could have pitched into the neighbour's garden with a wedge; opened the face, trusted to the loft of the club, floated the ball over the fence, drawn it up short with chirrup of backspin, softly, sweetly, miraculously. Very Tiger Woods. But when you're a wee boy confronted with a big bag of golf clubs, you instinctively reach for the one resembling a boxing glove on a stick.

Many years on, I found myself standing on the edge of the North Sea with my driver drawn and nothing to aim at but Scotland. The plan: to skelp a ball across the birthplace of the game, this time negotiating roads, towns, fields, rivers and mountains. I would tee off at Balmedie Beach, just north of my home in Aberdeen, and head for Loch Leven on the west-coast. And the par for this quarter-million yard course? Ten thousand, I reckoned, just over 60 strokes a mile.

# PAR 10,000

I wondered how people might react to a grown man driving, pitching, putting and hacking his way across their increasingly cramped country. I envisaged it as an expression of abandonment, an unashamedly mindless adventure. I would be someone quietly raging against the suffocating constraints of modern living. My pilgrimage: to rediscover the spirit with which I first let rip in the front garden. Reckless, maybe, but in his heyday so was Seve Ballesteros and everybody loved him for it.

As for that first drive, we never saw the ball again. My pals and I stood agog as it flew over the hedge, sheared past the house squatting behind it and dropped out of sight towards the driveway. We waited for the sound of breaking glass, the dull twang of punched steel, a scream, an ambulance siren. Thankfully, nothing came. I still haven't asked for the ball back. Sometimes you don't want to push your luck.

*David Ewen*
*April 2001*

# Golf: The Game

The aim of golf is to strike a small ball with a variety of clubs from the 'tee' across the 'fairway' to the 'green' and into the 'cup'. This should be done in as few shots as possible. A course comprises nine or eighteen of these 'holes'. The clubs include 'woods' (usually made of titanium), 'irons' (stainless steel) and the 'putter'. A 'two' iron, for example, is less lofted than a 'five' iron, producing a longer shot but a more shallow arc that makes the ball harder to control on landing. Most amateurs, however, are more concerned about getting the ball into the air. Modern clubs are heavily modified to help out, with oversized, offset heads that are weighted to reward imprecision. The putter is the most accurate club in the bag but is rarely used beyond the green. Many players would do better if they carried only a putter instead of the permitted fourteen clubs.

## ONE

# A Coo Will Tak' Yer Life

| HOLE 1 | DISTANCE: 3.5 MILES | PAR 219 |
| --- | --- | --- |

AS BUNKERS go, Balmedie Beach is one of the biggest around. It measures maybe 20 square miles, depending on what the North Sea is doing at the time. In contrast, the biggest bunker on the Old Course at St Andrews (named 'Hell') is around 500 square yards. Even Tiger Woods would struggle to clear Balmedie with a single shot. It's not just the swathe of sand that's the problem. There are other impediments too. Dogs, for example. Wind-surfers. Families and their barbecues. Because these obstacles often move about they make play unpredictable in the extreme. The Carnoustie rough may be long and tangled but at least it stays put.

For this reason I decided to tee off slightly to the north of the country-park, away from the day-trippers and their ball-chasing dogs. On a glorious May evening I found myself on Foveran links. For once the North Sea seemed utterly benign, petering out at the shore in series of short, breathless waves. A supply boat sat on the horizon where the blueness drained from the sky. I prefer this: sunset without the sun. Our nearest star is too much of a show-off at this time of day, suffusing the North-east hinterland with chintzy pinks and golds; cheap braid draped across the hills and fields. On the coast darkness creeps in like the haar, slowly fudging the boundaries between sky, sea and shore.

I pushed my tee into the damp, cocoa-coloured sand as the water lapped at my shoes. While it was firm enough to walk on, the first few inches folded like honey. The tee disappeared under the weight of the ball and I was forced to put my driver away. It's difficult enough to hit a number one wood from a juicy piece of fairway; flying the ball out of this brackish sludge wasn't on. I pulled a seven iron from my bag, a club with sufficient loft to get the ball airborne, but upright enough to give it a fair smack across the beach. As the surf receded I addressed the ball. I had about 30 seconds to make the shot before my feet got soaked.

It's always a big shot, that first one. Even when you're alone, it tickles the heart. It can set the tone for the whole round – in this case one lasting 160 miles. As a kid bent on breaking 50 at the local nine-hole course, I'd sometimes run back to the first tee and retake my place in the queue if I didn't hit a decent drive. Neurotic, yes, but golf is a game of tics. That wasn't an option now. I'd have to live with my drive wherever it went.

Standing shoogling over the ball, you become acutely conscious of the sounds around you. In the few seconds before contact, nature's most beguiling noises – waves shuffling sand, birds preparing to roost – can have all the appeal of an incontinent car alarm. There was no way I was going to get the sea and those bloody skylarks to shut up, so I just swung the club.

Not bad.

It wasn't the cleanest shot – the heavy, wet sand slowed the club head – but at least the ball left the earth. It arched across the beach and landed in a puff of dry sand, maybe 60 yards ahead.

*One.*

The second shot was much the same, another sluggish seven. Eight more shots took me to the dunes separating the beach from the fields beyond.

The narrow path leading between them was flanked by two unusually intimidating hazards. On the left there was a dung heap – great dollops of cow shit and straw laid out like cakes on a tray, garnished with coils of barbed wire. To the right there was a firing range, the sort of place where people go to discharge real guns.

A hook could have left me in the manure, and a slice with a .22 bullet in my brain.

My ball was wedged in a clump of marram grass, the tough thatch that holds the dunes together. I chose a sand-iron, hit it thin, skewed it left. The ball slammed into the dung.

Under the Rules of Golf, as approved by the Royal and Ancient Golf Club of St Andrews, a ball embedded in its own pitch mark may be 'lifted, cleaned and dropped without penalty, as near as possible to the spot where it lay but not nearer the hole'. If I'd been playing for The Open Championship I would have dived in, no question, and prised the ball free with my fingers, but there was no Claret Jug waiting at the end of this round. I hacked the ball free in three strokes, back towards some succulent young nettles, and from there managed to hit a long-iron into the first field.

*Thirteen.*

After the cement-like sand, the unyielding marram grass and the steamy embrace of manure, this was like a fairway. The neatly-chomped grass looked as if it belonged on a soldier's scalp. You could see your ball at 100 yards. Also dotted around were plenty of cow-pats, looking as if they'd been built by under-achieving moles.

Practising in a field as a boy, I had discovered these things go off like landmines; you take more than turf. The prospect of going home with cow crap in my hair didn't appeal. Preferred lies it was. (That is, the ball could be moved to a more suitable playing-spot near to where it landed.)

Two mid-range irons brought me to the edge of the next field, the one with the cows in it. Rather than dispersing at my arrival they gathered to watch, flocking to the fence like a crowd chasing a tournament leader. What should I do? Skirt them – or attempt to hit the ball over their heads?

By now the sun was low in the sky. A fantail of shredded white cloud caught its light, smearing it across the horizon, forcing me to squint. It was time to mark my ball's position and retire for the night.

*'A coo will tak' yer life.'* As he uttered these words, the farmer was smiling lazily. 'I've hid my ribs broken afore noo,' he said.

Anyone else might have thought he was joking. Having grown up in the North-east though, I knew he was serious; the teasing humour masks a public shyness. I'd gone to knock on the door of his big granite house before returning to my ball. Two green wellies stood outside, two fat black Labradors flapped around inside. There was a Land-rover in the driveway but the man who answered was as broad-spoken as they come.

Doric is a language unique to the North-east. Because of its Scandinavian origin it's often inscrutable to outsiders. The same is often said of the people who live here. On reaching these parts during a tour of Britain's coast, American travel writer Paul Theroux couldn't connect with Aberdeen. He first chanced upon an oil-rig which, 'looked like a mechanical sea monster defecating in shallow water . . . a symbol of this part of Scotland'. Theroux, you'll gather, didn't like the city. Indeed, in researching his book *The Kingdom by the Sea* he came to hate it more than any place he visited, this 'cold, stony-faced city . . . over-cautious and unwelcoming'.

From a man who has bedded down in the back streets of Bombay, that's pretty damning. Theroux blamed the city's surliness on its boom-town ego.

'Perhaps it has been made awful and was not naturally this way,' he wrote with breathtaking condescension.

We've always been a thrawn bunch. The parochialism I disliked as an adolescent now plays like an old music-hall joke. I find it wryly amusing, for example, that our airport is required to shut by 11.30 p.m. and must divert late planes hundreds of miles away despite no nearby resident having complained about noise.

I like the fact we don't bend to the wider world. Aberdeen Football Club was ready to host a Scottish international on the day of Princess Di's funeral until the Scottish Football Association lost its nerve and postponed the match. At first the club wanted to change it to another day but a couple had reportedly booked the stadium for their wedding and were refusing to give up their date. Don't you just love that?

I like the fact an incensed Theroux was turned away from a country-and-western nightclub because he was *wearing blue jeans*, and got told to 'piss off' when he haughtily suggested he might be Willie Nelson.

I also like farmers who won't give you a straight answer.

I'd explained to the farmer what I hoped to do; the scope of my odyssey in all its existential ambition. He looked at me without a word. I waited nervously, expecting him to declare his fields out of bounds.

'Hiv ye nithin' better tae dae wi' yer time?' he asked with an incredulous smile.

While the farmer was remarkably laid-back about the whole thing, he warned me his livestock might be less accommodating. 'Thir are een or twa bulls oot there . . .' Of course he wasn't he going to tell me which fields they were in.

'It's coos ye hiv tae worry aboot though,' he continued, now laughing. 'They're quicker than bulls. I've seen them toss a big bail of strae oot o the wye. They've some power, ye see. There's a ton-an-a-half ahin that heid. A coo will tak' yer life.' It was now starting to sound like a mantra. 'Especially if it's got a calf.'

'*Don't get between a cow and her youngster.*'

I'd heard this said of a grizzly bear but never a Friesian. What exactly do you do if you are accosted by an angry cow? Play dead? Make yourself as big as possible? Shake pepper in its face? 'Keep near tae the fence,' said the farmer.

On returning to the field I discovered he was right about the cows. They weren't there to cheer me on my way, but to moan and growl and intimidate like an American Ryder Cup crowd. They came from quarter of a mile away, crossing the field with surprising, unnerving pace, calves at their sides. They behaved like bulls, pawing at the ground, snorting and puffing and defying me to go for a club.

Until then 'playing safe' had meant laying the ball up short of a hazard or taking a shortened backswing in blustery conditions. Confronted with a field of belligerent cows, 'playing safe' becomes the difference between a warm bath at the end of the day and a trip to casualty. I aimed for a track running alongside the field. 'You could always stick to the paths,' the farmer had suggested. Perhaps his was an omnipotent laugh.

Playing along the dusty, knobbly track was taxing in itself, largely because the field on the other side also contained cows, although they did seem less truculent. I pitched and putted a few hundred yards, determined to keep the ball within the two fences, until I reached a second field on the right that contained only sheep. The farmer had said nothing about sheep and they appeared disinterested in golf.

As I climbed the gate I recalled that a farmer's wife had been killed by some sheep a few months earlier. They had driven her off a headland in southern England. Studying these animals, I was certain there was no premeditation or malice on the flock's part. Sheep have the dead, spooky eyes of a shark, but the fleshy, quivering mouth belongs to a drag queen. They didn't scare me.

The sheep moved away, hardly lifting their heads from the grass. Their green-keeping skills, however, were no match for the cows'. I lost six balls in one field before reaching an expanse of soil.

On a golf course you'll watch a wayward ball land, skitter into rough grass and you'll turn away to replace your club in the bag. You blithely assume you'll pick up the scent 200 yards down the fairway like some kind of bloodhound. But at close range one knot of grass can look much like any other. Ever eye-balled a television set and been amazed to find it's a collection of dots? Same thing here. From the tee you have an impressionist's view of your shot. The shapes and shadows delineating its position evaporate as you move closer. What often happens is that you find someone else's ball – not usually in a field of sheep, admittedly.

As a kid I used to forage for balls, a habit that persists today. If I'm passing some bushes, even on the poshest course, I'll always have a quick squint underneath. Espying a tiny white patch of Surlyn, wrapped in lacy weed . . . well, it still provides a measure of titillation, a sense that fate is smiling on you, especially if it's a pristine 'Top Flite' or 'Titleist' you unearth. Sometimes you will chance upon a ball sitting in the open, under a tree or even on a fairway, a miracle from heaven.

We would wash our balls and array them in egg boxes, same names together. There would be a hiatus when you could enjoy them like this. So perfect, so full of potential. And then the day would come when you had to take them back to the golf course and lose them all over again, dispatching them to the undergrowth for someone else to find.

Yes, hunting balls was often more exciting and rewarding than the golf itself. I wasn't having much luck in the sheep park, though. I resorted to an old technique: tap-dancing. Sure enough I felt the lump of a golf ball beneath my sole. Every third shot or so I had to make like Fred Astaire.

There was another snag too. Animals don't go to the bathroom. Here

I was, plunging my naked hand into the urine-soaked grass, groping around for an object the same shape and size as excrement.

The North-east has had several E.coli 0157 outbreaks, at least one of them linked to a sheep's backside. There is evidently a general problem with sundry faecal matter. Public health officials have since started to mutter about farms being no place for children – which leaves me wondering where farmers should raise theirs. In cages perhaps? Under water?

When I was at primary school we used to have boldly-coloured posters with titles like 'Animals you can see on the farm'. Cows, horses, sheep, chickens, butterflies, birds, all juxtaposed in ludicrous harmony, fox gamboling with poultry; cat with mouse. The health authorities are probably commissioning 'Diseases you can catch on the farm' as I write.

Maybe I should have gone for inoculations. In a way I was visiting a foreign land; I was putting my face squarely against Scotland's.

Our lives are not just sanitised but abstracted. From behind a fence a field is mere colour – green, brown, yellow. Walk across it, though, and you feel the day's residual heat rising from the soil. There's sound (wind stirring barely, a hare scrabbling for traction, a pewit fretting over her brood), smell (fragrant and malodorous), and above all, *choice*. There's no prescribed path. Hillwalkers make for the remotest part of this country only to follow blindly in another's footsteps. I was striking out across virgin pea field, breaking the baked earth my golf shoes, guided by a compass and the sun.

This Lawrence of Arabia fantasy dissolved when I reached the A975. It leaves a nearby trunk-road and leads to the coastal village of Newburgh. As I neared the verge I dropped my bag to the ground, trying not to catch any driver's eye. The traffic wasn't too heavy. All I had to do was wait.

A firmly struck seven – fast becoming a favourite club – carried me into the next field. More grass. Back to the wedge. Back to losing balls.

My hundredth shot took me into another field of earth, combed into foot-high furrows. Fortunately, the drills ran in a westerly direction and I was able to putt along them. Sometimes the ball would hop between tracks and I managed to lose one a foot from the field's edge.

The adjacent field was level and its cereal crop had only just surfaced. As I clambered between an avenue of short, thorny trees to reach it, a buzzard fell out of one. It flicked itself clear of the ground with a single beat of its wings, headed away, and then circled as if on a rope, perching on a nearby branch.

# PAR 10,000

Buzzard numbers have increased markedly in recent years and it now appears in suburban back-gardens along with kestrels and sparrow-hawks. People are invariably thrilled by this shaggy symbol of the wild, unaware the buzzard was once a city scavenger like the seagull, feeding on rubbish and copious vermin. Ornithologists are less pleased by its return. Having fought to protect birds of prey and boost their numbers, their new chant is 'save our songbirds' as finches and others succumb to the raptors.

The A90 carries nearly three 3,000 vehicles an hour during rush-hour. I stood at the roadside with my bag slung over my shoulder, buffeted by cars and lorries (and jeered by one van driver), considering my options. It was only prudent to allow myself a drop, anywhere along the A90's length but no nearer Loch Leven.

Once across I chose to follow a minor road and reached for the putter. Frankly, I'd had enough of grass and looking for balls. I expected this to be a red carpet ride but was wrong again. The first thing you discover about a road is that it isn't really flat. Your car may glide across it, cushioned by steel springs, but a golf ball reacts like a grasshopper. The surface is like the Rockies in miniature; protrusive chips launch the ball which then stoats around from side to side, springing ten feet in the air. Tarmac is also considerably quicker than any green. My first putt dived into the grass verge. I couldn't find the ball. I may have sworn. Yet again a canny approach was called for. A smooth putting stroke, not too forceful.

Occasionally cars would belt past as commuters rushed home to relax doing nothing. It was another balmy evening. A jet thrummed serenely overhead, its white belly margined with silver. Looking up I thought of the passengers aboard as bacteria in some giant bird's gut, greedily digesting food. They seemed far away, insignificant, like the sea now – and the hills I had yet to reach.

Far from being bored, I was enjoying the fields and byways. It was the immediate sights at hand I returned to, not the vistas. Bluebells of almost tropical brilliance; some kind of purple pansy I'd never noticed before. I stopped at Kincraig Farm. I'd come three miles in two hours, having lost nineteen golf balls on this fitful, disjointed opening hole. Seve would have surely approved.

**STROKES: 182     TOTAL: 182          SCORE: -37**

# *Scoring*

There are no leagues in golf but there is a 'handicap' system for amateurs. This equates to what you normally shoot over 'par' (this being the number of strokes a professional should take on a course, usually about 70 for an 18-hole). The maximum handicap is 28 for a man and 36 for a woman. In golf, a handicap provides an advantage. The bigger your handicap, the better off you'll be. Most club competitions are based on net scores (the actual score minus the handicap) which makes everyone feel like a professional and allows hackers to take cups home. But even with a handicap of 28 or 36 you can still become unstuck during stroke play. That's why many golfers prefer 'Match Play', 'Stableford' or 'Texas Scramble' which are based on points scored at individual holes. Under these formats you can take a million at the first hole, do well at the second, and still be in the lead. And that's before you've allowed for your handicap.

# TWO

# Ca' Canny wi' the Butter

| HOLE 2 | DISTANCE: 6 MILES | PAR 375 |
|---|---|---|

THE MODERN golf ball is a technical marvel. Titanium-reinforced shell for distance, tungsten centre for accuracy – it sounds like a piece of military hardware. Some of these balls could kill a human-being at 100 yards. But what I needed was a ball that would talk to me; something that would shout 'over here!' when I waded into the grass to look for it. I needed a ball with a built-in transmitter. To this end I approached the Dean of Engineering at Aberdeen University. Professor Jim Penman replied: 'I'm not sure what you are asking can be done very easily.' Keen to help though, he passed the request to my old professor of electronics, Tim Spracklen, in the hope he might produce a 'solution' which would make a Callaway Rule 35 look like a gutta-percha ball.

There was no point attempting this myself. When it came to engineering, I struggled with fundamental concepts. Engineering itself was one. Electricity was another. Maths had been my best subject at school but I wasn't so hot when it came to putting numbers in the equations. (Or more specifically, getting the right ones out.) I must have been one of the most undistinguished graduates to leave Aberdeen University in 500 years. When I was told someone in the department had built a 'Time Machine' my eyes had widened in wonder. 'A *model*,' stressed a friend, sparing his own blushes as much as mine. 'With flashing lights, like the one in the film.'

In addition to transmitting a homing signal, this super-ball would be able to record how often it was struck, how it was struck, and what distance it had travelled. All this information might be stored in an electronic chip and downloaded at the end of the trip. That much I did know. In the meantime I applied a daring piece of lateral thinking to the problem to produce a brilliant stop-gap . . . I would use a bright-green tennis ball.

A hollow sphere of vulcanised rubber might perhaps lack the high spin-rate of three-piece Balata or the ballistic acceleration of two-piece Surlyn, but who cares when it's so much easier to find? In long grass I couldn't afford to hit a golf ball more than 30 yards. I'd already lost 19 balls in 3 miles, dropping them like curious white stools. I was on course to surrender something like 1,000.

The real problem was the time I was spending looking for balls. Even if I'd been sponsored by a manufacturer and had an endless supply, I wouldn't have readily given up on a lost ball. I'd still have kicked around the grass, partly through habit, partly because of an ingrained sense of thrift.

The fields to the west of Kincraig Farm contained only soil. The owner, Ian Ross, gave me the thumbs up as he trundled by in a vehicle so outlandish he might have borrowed it from Judge Dredd. His lurcher followed me across the first field before a whistle drew him back.

I managed to cover lots of ground by placing the ball on a small clot of earth within a foot of where it landed (preferred lies, remember) and driving it as though from a tee. My own progress across the fields was less impressive. Clearing the drainage ditches was hard without the benefit of a five wood up my backside. Nettles hid lumpy ground; you risked twisting an ankle on landing or being stung lavishly if you braced your fall. You just had to arrive upright. Bag first, then golfer.

The Buchan countryside offers a startling panorama. Wind generators spin on hillsides like disembodied plane propellers. Vast, cigar-shaped silos – used to make animal feed – point towards the sky, as if ready to blast off.

Generations of farmers laboured to make Buchan arable, to clear it of all but the very biggest boulders. These car-sized rocks still lie about the fields here, unmolested by modern machines, each a monument to graft. Drystone dykes were built with the smaller stones to provide protection from the winds whipping off the North Sea, but even now much of the land can't support cereal crops, only grass for grazing. Buchan feels like desert.

One thing about golf – it shrinks the globe. The fields stretch interminably towards the horizon, to the point at which the planet itself curves out of sight. Knock a golf ball in front of you and that becomes the horizon. It's the psychological equivalent of cutting steps in a slope. Golf isn't a 'good walk spoiled', as Mark Twain suggested, but 'a long walk shortened'.

I'd hit a couple of slices and lost both balls but remained well within par. Eventually the earth gave way to thin, glossy grass which squeaked underfoot. As I pulled out an eight iron, I was conscious of a four-wheel-drive vehicle passing and reversing on the farm track behind me. A young man got out and stood by the fence, hands on hips, waiting for some sort of enlightenment. I downed the club and jogged towards him, trying to appear as subservient as possible.

'Can I help you?' he said.

Magnus Sinclair farmed this field and 800 acres besides. His manner softened when I explained what I was up to and he was happy to chat.

'Don't go into the field with the cows, there's a bull there,' he said as I described the rest of the day's route. 'He's a nasty piece of work. He *will* kill you. He doesn't even like the dairyman. And watch out for the fence, it's electric. It will knock you to the ground a bit. You'll also have to cross a burn. Head for that clump of trees. There's a bridge.'

Gored, electrocuted, drowned – suddenly golf was up there with pot-holing and base-jumping in the danger sport stakes.

Granny Sinclair, who lived in the house near the field, I was told, had settled in the North-east in the 1950s. The farm's main business was dairy production. Milk was fetching a paltry thirteen pence a litre but that didn't keep supermarkets from selling it for four times the price, something that riled Magnus. During the BSE crisis, supermarkets were able to buy British beef at rock-bottom prices. Shelf prices, however, stayed high, making farmers feel exploited and resentful. Farmers believe the Government has failed to protect both their interests *and* those of the consumer in recent years.

'We produce wheat that's cheaper than North America's but we still import it,' said Magnus, sounding bewildered. 'There's always a hidden agenda.'

Like many farmers, Magnus has been forced to diversify. Three hundred acres of his family's land now supports forestry.

Golf too has become a new crop. In the summer of 1999, East Aberdeenshire Golf Centre opened a few miles south of the Sinclair farm. It took £1.5 million to transform 130 acres of prime arable land into an 18-hole course. The owner, David Watson, is from a farming family but had already diversified into haulage before giving his fields over to golf. He had always wanted to own a course – although strangely he has no desire to play the game.

Ian Creswell, a former branch president of the Scottish Golf Union and Director of Golf here, designed it.

'I learned about course architecture when I was green convener at Westhill Golf Club,' he said. 'Once I had the sniff of grass in my nostrils, that was it. I've taken every thought I've had about every course I've played over the years, good bits and bad. I was out there when the bulldozer went to work, using my thumb . . . I'd say "take a wee bit here, a wee bit there". It was a dream come true.'

Construction, carried out by specialists Glen Andrews, took nine months. A survey of homes within a 5-mile radius of the course had shown 700 people were interested in joining. Membership (£340 enrolment, £340 annual green fees) stands at just 400, not that the Director of Golf is worried.

'I thought with Tiger Woods we would have seen more people taking up golf,' said Ian. 'I can only think it's down to the oil recession and job insecurity. People don't want to part with the guts of £1,000 to play golf when they might be out of work the following year.'

Another new course opened last year, built on land owned by the Scottish College of Agriculture with a £500,000 lottery grant.

'Now you can get into a club in five minutes,' said Ian. 'It was never like that in my day.'

His grandfather helped found Calley Golf Club and his dad also played. Ian is 66, has arthritis in both knees, but still keeps his golf handicap down to 6 which means he is only a handful of shots behind a club professional.

'I've haven't been that high since 1957,' he said with disgust. For 20 years he played to professional standard and won just about every competition in the North-east. 'I thought about playing for a living but my father had a big plumbing business and there was more money in plumbing then.'

Tiger Woods' take-home pay was thirty million pounds in 1999.

I pictured Ian playing East Aberdeenshire. I imagined him craning into the wind, dragging his ageing body up the ever-steepening hills, pitting himself against his own creation, proud of the challenge but too proud to let it get the better of him just yet.

'I don't think I've ever completed a round,' he said without sentiment. 'East Aberdeenshire is work.'

To behold the greenery of a golf course, to learn about the birds and animals which walk its fairways at dusk and dawn, to listen to TV commentator Peter Alliss describing the game in reverential, lullaby tones . . . you can easily forget golf is a sport, played by some ruthless people who want only to win, people who care only for a cash prize and not the more ethereal pleasures golf brings.

Golfers don't engage in direct contact with opponents but the aggression of the best – the urge to lock horns and crush contemporaries – boils as strongly as it does in footballers, boxers and racing drivers, and is manifest in the swing itself. Golf is a game of extraordinary violence. When Tiger Woods smashes a ball 320 yards off the tee – a 'red-ass special' as he calls it – the club impacts at 132 mph.

'I'm naturally competitive – I've got to win – and golf was the only sport I was any good at,' said Ian. 'I only play by myself to improve. A poor player comes off the course thinking about all the good shots he's played; a good player thinks about all the bad shots he's played. I've walked off courses because I'm playing badly, not striking the ball the way I want to, not getting it to go where I want it to.

'I want new knees now so I can play in competitions again, but the doctor has said I'll have to wait until I'm 70.'

There was no point asking Ian for a game. 'I'd rather go to the dentist than play a bounce game with a high handicapper,' he said. 'Golfers shouldn't be given more than a stroke a hole in competitions but that doesn't happen because the people in power, on committees and so on, haven't played golf to a high standard.'

Ian is no elitist. True, he likes to see club members in a collar and tie and finds the thought of a woman captaining a golf club novel in the extreme, but he is determined to make everyone welcome at East Aberdeenshire. Like many new golf clubs, it is being promoted as a family experience – a place with a restaurant and a bar and plenty of practice areas. Ian is planning to create a six-hole par-three course for beginners, whatever their gender or predilection in dress. Everyone is equal on the first tee.

'Nobody cares what you are when you're on a golf course.'

It was time to bring out the tennis ball. The Buchan grass had become as deep and as thick as snow in places.

The first few shots travelled only a few feet, the club sliding under the ball and sending it skywards. Joyfully, it sat on top of the grass, my very own bouncing bomb. I didn't have to fixate on the spot where it landed. I could at last lift my head between shots, turn my face towards the warm sun as I walked across the fields. And then it happened. The thing went missing behind enemy lines.

I rummaged among the grass with increasing desperation, thrashing around in all directions. The grass was long enough to carry footprints, allowing me to backtrack to where I first started my search, but after 25 minutes I gave up on recovering the ball. There was now every chance I would run out of golf balls before I reached the village of Pitmedden. My tube of 20 was already half empty.

The next field had sheep in it and was a lawn in comparison. I climbed a big pile of boulders (another shrine to hard work) and checked my scorecard. Two miles, sixty-four shots. Well below par. I was hot, hungry and glad of the breeze. The wind fanned a field of young barley, which rippled like a shoal of fish. A house sat on the slope above. It had quartered windows, two tall chimneys, the sort of boxy functionality you find in a child's drawing. Blobby trees surrounded it; the sun was smiling; I was the stick man in the foreground.

# CA' CANNY WI' THE BUTTER

Fine compacted soil formed a border around the barley, allowing me to cut corners by thumping the ball high over the crop.

Pieces of drainage pipe lay underfoot. When a tractor churns a field it churns the past, exhuming the remnants of a bygone life. Years ago there wasn't a weekly refuse collection. People used to toss their rubbish in a dump near their houses. In ploughed fields I've found broken crockery, the stem of a clay pipe, the neck of an ancient ginger beer bottle stout enough to anchor a ship.

'You're a long way from a golf course,' a cheerful woman remarked as I putted past her house after crossing the bridge. I left the road after 400 yards for a field where last season's cut barley poked between weeds like stubble. More tilled soil followed, bringing more opportunities to use the wood. I reached the settlement of Logierieve on a splendid 138.

The B9000 was my undoing. I asked if I could play in a field running parallel with the road and a farmer's young son had said 'yeh, go for it'. He didn't think to mention the cows.

They came stampeding over a rise, arriving from behind in a welter of snorting and seismic foot-stamping. When I first swung round, I couldn't be sure there wasn't a bull among them. It was a scary moment – and Magnus Sinclair's dairyman wasn't around to save me. The cows drew up short. I walked slowly towards my ball. They followed. I played a very gentle wedge, keeping my head up, and gingerly climbed the barbed-wire-fence near where my ball had landed.

Most of the other roadside fields contained either livestock or knee-high barley. Some of the cows had what looked like raffle tickets pinned to their ears, making them look punkish. Friesians shape up as four-legged killer whales – they share the same markings. I stuck to the B9000.

The road was reasonably straight, flat and quiet. I swung the putter with one hand, using the camber to bring the golf ball back to my side. It bobbled along like some bizarre Japanese tech-pet you might take for a walk.

A farm road offered a short-cut to Pitmedden. The long driveway was edged with gasping red tulips and white posts. Two milk churns topped with shrubs stood at the entrance to the house.

Again, I felt like I was abroad. That's when you find yourself staring at the most mundane things – coins, cutlery, buses, taps, stamps, electrical fittings, food packaging. You're alive to new sights and smells and tastes and sounds. You're ready to make new friends. It's like revisiting your childhood. I was about to knock on a stranger's door and ask if I could play golf in the garden. It felt exciting.

Regrettably, the woman who answered didn't really share my zeal. She suggested coming back in autumn, after the barley had been harvested. I asked about an empty field.

'We're about to put tatties in there,' she said. 'Besides, the ground's undulating.' I explained that I was heading for the National Trust's Museum of Farming Life at Pitmedden Garden. (The subtext: I'm interested in farming; I'm sympathetic to your way of life; I will highlight your difficulties to the world.) 'You'll get some golf at Pitmedden Garden,' she continued helpfully. 'Just follow the main road and turn right at the junction.'

She just didn't get it. It wasn't until I turned and walked back to the main road that I considered this disappointing exchange from her perspective. Here was a grimy man with a bag of golf clubs and a garish headband, asking if he could let rip across her tattie field. On reflection I should have been thankful she didn't call the police.

I reached Pitmedden in 232 shots. I decided not to play through the village but to treat it as 'free drop' – sensible given that it was a Saturday afternoon.

One of the first sights you encounter here is a public toilet – square, flat-roofed and harled. An unremarkable building you might think, unlikely to instil any great sense of civic pride or devotion. You'd be wrong. The local authority had just shut this and 68 other loos in a bid to save £316,000 from its annual budget, incensing the people of Pitmedden and elsewhere. They staged a sit-in at the local authority's headquarters in Aberdeen, occupying toilet cubicles. Paul Theroux would have been unimpressed.

The local youngsters aren't so respectful of this municipal wonder. The toilet windows have been stoned are there's graffiti scrawled across the locked door: *Only smarties have the answer*. This is more likely to be a reference to ecstasy ('smarties' is a nickname for the drug) than to Cadbury's dinky chocolate sweets. Drugs, of course, are found in nearly every town and village now. In some of parts of the country they are reportedly sold from ice-cream vans ('give us a slider and couple of E's'), though not, it should be said, in Pitmedden.

The fishing town of Fraserburgh, about 20 miles to the north, has among the highest number of heroin addicts per capita in Scotland – as many as one in five young men. Mothers dread their sons returning from the sea because they now face greater danger on land. Five years ago fishermen spent their cash on a fast car. Some have sold their cars to pay for their smack. (Even some of their nicknames have changed; they're no longer redolent of the sea but of the drugs scene.) In the past fisherfolk trusted to God – He alone could save them in a tempest – and this has made them somewhat fatalistic, though that is changing. Really, though, Fraserburgh isn't so different from anywhere else. It's big enough for its statistics to stand out, but too small and isolated to hide its problem, its people too blunt to try.

On the far side of Pitmedden I dropped my ball at the 30 mph speed limit sign, chipped it along a tree-lined path, over two fields and through a sun-dappled beech wood. Another 33 shots.

The Museum of Farming Life is place of horror. It hosts a collection of machinery and artefacts dating from 1880 to the Second World War. There aren't any £50,000 turbo-charged tractors here, instead there are some tools that look like they might have come from a cave.

The farm workers around here were transients who lived in a bothy, recreated at the museum. It comprises a single room with a box-bed and fireplace, and makes a prison cell seem like a penthouse. On the mantle-piece sits a packet of rat poison carrying a cheery promise to 'sweep it all away'. A dummy has been laid in the bed – mouth open, eyes screwed shut, head titled back as though gasping his last, flesh livid in the shadows. It looks like a cadaver and made me jump. But perhaps he was meant to be dead.

God shows up, reproachfully, in the farmer's house. In the lounge there's a bible the size of a breeze-block: a moral anchor. Above the marital bed, the one place where you might loose yourself a bit, where any seed-sowing might actually be fun, hangs an embroidered sign: 'Bring your sins and sorrow here'. That's a mood killer to rank alongside farting under the duvet. In spring, farm workers used to spend their day behind a horse-drawn plough, sowing the crops by hand. In summer they hoed turnips and made hay. In autumn they turned themselves into a combine harvester. And in winter they would pull up the turnips (again by hand) to feed the cattle. It was a routine of back-breaking drudgery, fuelled with a diet of oatmeal and relieved only by a sing-song at night spent recalling the shit day they'd had – presumably some kind of catharsis.

The most astounding thing of all is the stoicism with which people bore this finger-shredding, oppressive way of life. They rarely complained and even appeared genuinely contented, perhaps because there simply wasn't time to be unhappy. They were at constant war with the land, after all; the singular, consuming purpose in life was to subjugate it to their rule. Today, around one-third of Scotland's cereal crop is produced on the east-coast.

On a jug in the farmer's house there's a poem:

> Let the wealthy and great roll in splendour and state
> I envy them not I declare it
> I eat my own lamb, my chicken and ham
> I shear my own fleece and I wear it
> I have lawns I have bowers, I have fruit I have flowers
> The lark is my morning alarmer
> So my jolly boys now, here's God speed the plough
> Long life and success to the farmer

This could have been romanticism or propaganda. There was another line, dancing across a small dish, which for me better encapsulates the North-east character: 'Ca' canny wi' the butter.' This was a telling-off disguised as a caution – revealed only after you had gobbled the butter.

**STROKES: 265      TOTAL: 447      SCORE: -147**

# *The Rules of Golf*

'Salamander' is the common name for about 300 species of tailed amphibian. They are usually four to six inches long and brightly coloured, often brown, black, yellow, or red, and have spots or stripes. They are found mainly in the temperate regions of the Northern Hemisphere, near water and damp places. Some live in trees, others in holes in the ground where they may leave distinctive footprints and droppings. And why do you need to know this? Because if your ball lands in a hole made by a burrowing animal such as a salamander, rabbit, mole or gopher this is treated as 'abnormal ground conditions', and under Rule 25-1 you're entitled to a free drop. Most golfers break the rules every time they play. Want to know what club a friend is using? If he's not your partner in a competition, you lose two strokes for asking, under Rule 8-1. And when the world's best take five hours to complete a round, they are probably breaching 'slow play' guidelines set out under Rule 6-7 by the course committee.

# THREE

# Animal Farm

| HOLE 3 | DISTANCE: 6 MILES | PAR 375 |
|--------|-------------------|---------|

ABOUT A YEAR ago I played Forres (the 18-hole golf course that is, not the town). It was beyond my ability: there are par-fours I struggle to reach in two woody shots. Ninety would be a dandy score. After four holes I was just two over par and grew increasingly excited, giddily trotting between holes, extrapolating wildly, anxious to consolidate. Breaking 80 looked like a real possibility. But of course the low scoring didn't last. At the fifth, a par-three, I dropped it in the bunker, put the next shot over the back of the green and ended up taking seven.

Really, I should have seen it coming. Somewhere, sooner or later, I was going to muck up in a major way. We can all play shots that would have Tiger Woods punching the air with satisfaction. On a football pitch, every Sunday league player will make a pass of sublime artistry – but usually once every two or three years. Quality is nothing without consistency. The law of averages always conspires against you in the end.

As I left Pitmedden Garden, I was doing the sums. Two holes; two days of temperate weather, benevolent farmers, reasonable fairways. In theory I had an evens chance of the same again. Cumulatively, I was waiting for it to all go wrong.

I pitched my way off the National Trust property, playing along a wide grass verge, and within a few shots dropped the ball on the entrance road where it bounced out onto the A920. It hung in the air, just waiting to collect a car. If one struck it at 60 mph the damage would be substantial – much like taking a Big Bertha to the bonnet.

In this game you don't need a good caddie but you do need a good solicitor. Staying out of jail is more important than staying out of the rough. Before I'd set off, I had consulted Ewen Roy, one of the country's finest young criminal briefs. He is ambitious but methodical, having worked for both the procurator fiscal's office in Glasgow and as a defence solicitor pioneering a new form of legal aid in Edinburgh.

He had explained that anybody injured on a golf course falls under the Latin maxim *volenti fit non injuria*. That is, you accept you may get brained.

'If, on the other hand,' said Ewen, 'I'm getting out the morning papers on the high street and a golf ball comes from nowhere knocking me arse over tit, then I've got a right to get a bit miffed and my remedy in law is to sue the golfer.'

In Scotland it isn't a criminal offence to trespass on someone's land. According to Ewen, I could 'simply jeer' at the traditional warning sign announcing, 'trespassers will be prosecuted'. A landowner could go to the Sheriff Court to obtain an interdict to keep me out, but was fairly unlikely to do so unless I was planning to set up permanent camp or stage a rock concert.

'The farmer is more likely to shout "get off my land!" before setting the hounds on you, but at least you'll have the satisfaction of knowing you're right,' said Ewen. As the person in line for the bite on the bum, I didn't find this altogether reassuring.

What's more, I could get arrested if I destroyed property, including fences and crops. The charge would be 'malicious mischief', or vandalism. There must be a 'deliberate wicked intent to injure another or his property . . . or a deliberate disregard of, or even indifference to the property of others'. In *Ward* v *Robertson* (1938) a trespasser who had trampled some grass was acquitted because the court reckoned he wasn't to know it was a growing crop. There was no way I could pretend to mistake serried ranks of sweet peas or barley for anything other than a crop.

It wasn't just barley I stood to flatten though. There were people out there. In 1998 a man was charged with recklessness after firing a high-calibre rifle at a target in a wood near a public road. He was carrying out an accuracy test ('damn it, missed') on a weapon that could kill at three miles. Similarily, if I cracked a one wood near 'a number of members of the public' I could get done for 'endangering life and limb', even if the ball failed to connect with flesh. All it would take would be two witnesses.

Even if I didn't actually injure anybody, I could still be held to be negligent and end up getting sued for damages in a civil court where the burden of proof isn't so great. In the case of some crazy ricochet, the pursuer would still have his work cut out, though. Let's say I hit a seagull that falls from the sky and smashes a car windscreen, causing the driver to crash. Any action by him would probably fail. That's because the odds on the bird–car strike are astronomical, and not 'reasonably foreseeable' according to Ewen. If, on the other hand, I cracked a cow's skull open with the ball, I'd probably have to shell out compensation *and* get taken away in a police van.

Ewen reckoned I would be okay 'just about anywhere' with the putter. 'If you don't want to get sued,' he said, 'avoid people and built-up areas. Otherwise practice, practice, practice.'

Leaving Pitmedden Garden, though, I was fortunate: the ball ended up in the gutter.

The air was flecked with rain, the sky sullen, but the gorse lining the fields still blazed like an over-decorated Christmas tree. The first mile was easy going, on earth and then grass. I'd adopted a new technique, aiming for discrete targets such as a clump of dockens or the edge of a wall. I would fire a six-iron over the thickest grass, straight for a patch of worn ground by a gate, viewing it as a green isolated by water.

The land ahead was quite different – softer, rolling, less barren. Plants appear to cling to the bare back of Buchan, whereas in Formartine the shoulder of one field braces another against the wind, forming a protective huddle. Beech trees – not scratty bushes – rise between, ranged like umbrellas against the rain and sun. Crops are cradled among the folds. Formartine is a land of bosoms.

I marked my ball to take a look at Tolquhon Castle, a ruin that retains its original majesty. It is surrounded by graveyard grass (manicured yet full of daisies) and lugubrious yew trees from which it rises like the Cuillin of Skye. You find yourself plotting routes along its high, serrated walls. The oldest part, a tower, was built by Sir John Forbes more than 500 years ago, 'probably for his wife Marjorie'.

Back in the fields a helicopter chuntered overhead, ferrying oil workers back to Aberdeen Airport. The offshore industry has proved as moody as the North Sea, stirred by vast economic forces, its peaks and troughs tossing people in and out of work. Many have lost their jobs and found themselves re-employed in the same position with the same company as a contractor. They often get paid more. The illusion of being better-off can last until their first long holiday or a bout of sickness, when no money comes in, or until their computer sets fire to the house and they discover there's no business cover on their insurance.

When the price of crude halved in 1999, around 10,000 people lost their livelihoods – rig workers, those running the guest-houses in which they stayed, people in support industries. I know of one family — mother, father, son – who all lost their jobs with the same helicopter operator, the one that owned the machine passing above.

Fifty-seven strokes brought me to the first house. I asked the owner if I could play over his land and he invited me in. Robert Rothney's father had been a farmer but he chose to go to college and become a civil servant. Although officially retired, he was still working part-time at the Department of Agriculture, handing out some of the half-billion-pound European Union support paid to Scotland's 12,600 full-time and 16,000 part-time farmers each year.

Every country needs food, which is why people around the world are given Government help to grow things. If farming wasn't worthwhile financially, nobody would bother with it and we'd all go hungry. The EU was determined to be self-sufficient in food and its Common Agricultural Policy has topped up farmers' incomes with a defence-sized budget for many years. Farmers receive a payment over and above what they get for produce, based on the crop acreage or number of animals they own.

If anything the policy has been too successful. To reduce support being paid out, the EU introduced a 'set-aside' ruling which requires big farms to leave some of their arable land fallow – 10 per cent in Scotland's case. Fishermen, too, are constrained in what they can harvest. In the North-east they used to worry about catching too few fish. Now they worry about catching too many. Anything above the EU quota is returned to the sea dead, or sold on the corrosive black market.

The agricultural support system is often hugely abused. In Italy farmers have been in the habit of borrowing each other's livestock to claim double their payment. In 1998 the agriculture ministry in Rome revealed that nearly half of the million sheep, goats and cattle on which Italy's farmers claimed support didn't actually exist. Attempts to make satellite checks on the size of olive groves – the biggest scam of all – is frustrated by the use of plastic trees.

The policy also appears to be somewhat perverse. Richard Goldsworthy, a Welsh farmer, was paid £15,000 in support over several years to produce a crop nobody wanted. Rather than spending £1,300 harvesting linseed fibre flax destined to be destroyed, he dug it back into the ground – and was promptly charged with obtaining the EU cash by deception. He ended up being fined £1,500 at Swansea Crown Court.

Farmers themselves these days are no better off, certainly in Scotland. Present EU support, calculated in Euros, barely covers production costs. The strong pound has devalued aid, made selling abroad increasingly hard and allowed cheap imports to flood the domestic market. Yet while wheat grown in Scotland fetches the same price it did 25 years ago, the price of a loaf of bread is noticeably more than it was in 1975.

Like many, Robert Rothney believes the 'shareholders of the supermarkets' are getting rich while farmers go bankrupt. In a policy document, The National Farmers' Union of Scotland has described supermarkets as behaving 'to the detriment of supplier and not necessarily to the benefit of consumers' and has said that 'even if there is no proven abuse of monopoly power, as sellers of groceries there has been a deliberate exercise of buying power'.

Farming incomes have plummeted in the last five years. Scottish Enterprise Grampian has warned that the number of farmers in the North-east could drop by a fifth within the next three years. Jim Walker, president of the National Farmers' Union of Scotland, believes we have reached 'a defining moment in the history of Scottish agriculture'. Meanwhile, the Common Agricultural Policy appears to have become a giant money-laundering exercise.

The World Trade Organisation wants to curtail farming support linked to production because they say it corrupts free trade. In future direct support will almost certainly end and farmers will be on a retainer for keeping land in agricultural use. The National Farmers' Union of Scotland accepts the need for change, but wants it to be gradual. Its policy document states:

> The CAP – which has been a market-manipulating tool – is changing. And people expect agriculture to provide more than just food. Future policy must take account of the multifunctional role of agriculture – provider of food, cornerstone of rural communities and custodian of the environment. Government

cannot any longer control the levers of supply and demand. So to achieve the public benefits of farming, an active role in agricultural support by the UK and Brussels should remain.

At the moment only the high price of land keeps the banker at bay. If that collapses, traditional farming in Scotland could end. There's concern that farms will be swallowed up by massive wholesale organisations. Because they buy fertilisers and machinery direct from the manufacturers, local businesses could fold. Many people fear rural economies could crumble and a whole way of life may disappear. The land itself would then change, reverting to its wild state. Abandoned isolated holdings will be reclaimed by scrub. A century's worth of toil will count for nothing.

'There will only be tourism,' said Robert.

He sold the family farm but retained 85 acres, which is set-aside. Farmers can create voluntary 'set-aside' for which they receive support close to that for growing crops.

'In the '60s and '70s it was all about production . . .' he said wistfully. 'But I can see both sides of the coin now. Set-aside is good for a small farmer. I had rented the farm out for while and had no machinery. I would have had to buy some or get a contractor in if I wanted to grow crops, and that just wouldn't have been profitable.'

The uncultivated field in front of his house filled up with clover, then buttercups. Ten years on there's ball-gobbling grass. 'I used to play a bit of golf myself,' he said. 'I've lost a few balls in that field.'

His set-aside did indeed swallow three golf balls and a tennis ball in quick succession. I sent up a curlew which wheeled over the grass, piping as it went – the sound of approaching dusk. At the foot of the field, just over the dyke, a watering hole had formed. Cow shit lay around it like beached jellyfish, covered in flies. Some of the shit had mixed with mud; I was up to my ankles. The law of averages was beginning to prevail.

After 105 shots I reached Mains of Cairnbrogie, one of several farms owned by Arthur Simmers, Scotland's biggest pig producer. More than 70 per cent of the country's pigs live in the North-east but the numbers halved in 1999. When the market collapsed, 600 jobs were lost. Because 10 per cent of their crop went to pigs, cereal producers suffered too. Ancillary industries trembled. One North-east haulier saw his turnover drop by £70,000 in 6 months.

It wasn't that everybody suddenly went off bacon. During the slump, pig imports actually rose by more than 40 per cent in 6 months – and many of them had been reared in a cheap manner now illegal here.

Adverts for British pork have played on the barbarity of growing a pig in a tiny stall ('18 inches – the longest walk this pig will make') and have urged consumers to 'look after the farmers who look after their pigs'. In this country some farmers even rub sun-tan lotion on their animals – though they presumably stop short of bringing them an iced-drink at midday. Can you imagine the French slapping *Ambre Solaire* on their sows?

The Amnesty International-type tactics did appear to be working. Business was picking up. Arthur Simmer's empire crashed in 1998 but he had since bought it back from the receiver.

Mains of Cairnbrogie carried a warning sign: KEEP OUT. PLEASE DO NOT ENTER THESE PREMISES TO PROTECT THE WELL-BEING OF THE PIGS ON THIS FARM.

A man stood by a tractor, turning taps and running off some liquid from a tank behind it.

'I'm only here to do a job,' he said, giving nothing away. He seemed to be the only person about. It all felt very B-movie.

I turned back, past the front of a cavernous concrete hangar and continued along its side. The barley in the field here was too mature to golf in. Even the tractor tracks were overgrown. The heavy, wet sheaves licked at my legs; it was like wading across a burn. I had to pick up the ball up and incur a penalty – 50 strokes for the length of the field.

As I continued past the hangar, I became aware of abstruse noises escaping between the wooden slats – a discord of banging, thrashing, whining and groaning. The building was as big as a factory. Listening again, I thought the calls sounded drunken and debauched rather than pained and agitated. But these pigs were the ones inside. *I* was the one blundering through the dubs and the rain and the fading light.

I had to scramble up a small rubbish dump at the field's end, over blackened bed-springs, nettles and pieces of corrugated iron which slid over one another and threatened to slice off my foot. During the Open at Carnoustie in 1968, John Morgan was bitten by a rat while addressing his ball; I felt similarly exposed here. Beyond the dump a tribe of cows with blood-shot eyes gathered behind a flimsy fence, shepherded up by a deep-chested bull. Turning south towards the farm track, I expected to find the pigs on the far side of the hangar smoking cigars, driving tractors, drinking cocktails – maybe even practising golf. An irate, gun-totting Arthur Simmers would have been a joy to behold. But as I turned the corner there was no one there.

Bennachie rose in the distance, its distinctive shape smudged a little by melting cloud, and this cheered me a fraction. I pitched along the sandy road, stepping between a plague of black slugs, and quickly came upon a dilapidated croft. Broken windows and rusting machinery hinted at an experiment gone wrong. Gavin Maxwell, author of *Ring of Bright Water*, described loneliness as a lack of connection: you actually need people around you to feel alienated. So it was with this forsaken small-holding. It was desolate in a way mountains never are. It represented human failure; a scurrying retreat from some apocalyptic event.

I wanted to get away from this malevolent place and tried to play across some marsh, promptly sinking in to my knees. An earth field lay to the left and I incurred another 50-stroke penalty to reach it. The marsh water squelched around in my shoes. A toe-nail had nicked the flesh on one foot; I imagined pig swill flooding the open cut, carrying streptococcus straight to my heart. (Two days earlier I had read about a farmer with a weak constitution who had died, it was thought, after being *breathed* on by a pig.)

I decided to follow tracks all the way to Oldmeldrum, which was still two miles away. The sense of foreboding persisted. I then managed to mistake some sheep for pigs, making an unnecessary diversion. After these hallucinations came disembodied voices. When a farmer passed on his tractor, I heard a group of people cackling behind me, swung round, and saw only his backside. He had the radio on in his cab but I hadn't heard it above the engine at the front.

Putting along a tarmac road is tedious. I wanted to complete the hole another day (if at all) and tried hitching a lift, but nobody stopped. I guess a putter isn't the best thing to wave a car down with.

And then, mercifully, I came upon Oldmeldrum Golf Course. Holes 15, 16 and 17 – 'Fairways', 'The Laird' and 'Mither Tap' – run alongside the road. I pitched onto the course, just behind a family of four. The six-iron twisted in my wet, limp hands and the ball careered back across the road, disappearing forever into the field beyond it. Eventually the town came into view. It spread out below – a church spire poking up between trees, lights flicking on in homes. The sun was partly obscured by a bloated purple cloud, behind which it sunk like a lazy eye in the sky. A sign outside the clubhouse said 'No chipping' but for me the rules had changed irrevocably. A downhill putt took me charging past the 30 mph sign and into Oldmeldrum, my 344th shot. It had been one hellish walk through the crushing green fields of Formartine . . .

**STROKES: 334      TOTAL: 781      SCORE: -188**

# Origins of the Game

Like many sports, golf grew out of our base love of hitting things, especially with sticks. In the fourteenth century the Dutch gave this impulse a name – kolf – but failed to secure a copyright. The name 'golf' officially derives from the Lowland Scots word 'gowff', meaning 'to strike'. The game was played in Scotland during the fifteenth century and was so popular that James II passed an Act of Parliament banning it. He was worried it would keep people from practising their archery, an altogether more useful skill when it came to repelling enemies of the kingdom.

Golf, then, was the first truly pointless pastime.

# FOUR

# A Sprinkling of History

THE ROYAL and Ancient defines 'casual water' as: 'any temporary accumulation of water on the course which is visible before or after the player takes his stance and is not a water hazard'. From where I was standing this was a pretty fair description of the first few fields immediately to the west of Oldmeldrum. Storm clouds ran like mascara across the blue sky; teeming rain had turned the land around me into a paddy-field.

Under Rule 25-1(b):

> The nearest point of relief is the reference point for taking relief without penalty from interference by an abnormal ground condition. It is the point on the course, nearest to where the ball lies, which is not nearer the hole and which, if the ball were so positioned, no interference (as defined) would exist. The player should determine his nearest point of relief by using the club he expects to play his next stroke to simulate the address position and swing for such a stroke.

In other words, I was entitled to a free drop. Fortunately the map showed a 'dismantled railway' marginally to the west of the saturated ground and so I decided to play from there. Under the same rule I could also clean my ball, but I didn't fancy getting cow shit on my fleece.

There was a fishery at the roadside, not much bigger than a puddle. Half a dozen anglers stood on the bank, spread out like garden gnomes. Just what was going on there? Half the fun of fishing is wondering what's on the end of your line. When I was a kid I used to drop a worm into a burn where it met the River Dee. From this churning brown lucky-bag you could pull out brown trout, sea trout, pike, perch, eel, flounder or salmon. Fishermen at stocked lochs usually take home four or six identical-sized rainbow trout, gutted and wrapped. That's not angling. That's shopping. The biggest fish are sometimes given names. These are invariably returned to the water to be caught over and over ('see you next week, Archie'). A fishery makes men as dumb as trout: both are lured with artificial rewards.

The railway track was overgrown but playable, the two sleeper marks still discernible amongst the high grass, sticky-willies and other riotous vegetation. I was nursing a bruised Achilles tendon (caused by new golf shoes) and was sporting 'desert boots' – about as clever as wearing a pair of wellies in the Sahara. While they're delightfully soft on the skin, they're no more waterproof than slippers. But that's why you go to the countryside – to get wet and cold and burned and bitten and slapped about a bit. Still, I wouldn't have refused a pair of hermetically-sealed Gore-tex socks as I sloshed my along the track.

This, I suspect, was once a branch line running off the main Aberdeen–Inverness route. Many rail services in the area were axed during Dr Beeching's 'reforms' of the 1960s. The name still provokes rancour in the North-east, and must do throughout rural Britain where train travel would again be popular if only somebody hadn't torn up all the tracks. (The truth, however, is that many of these lines actually closed between the two World Wars when people switched to the newfangled bus and car.)

I used a nine-iron, aiming for the tuft of grass in the track's centre. It was possible to find a decent lie but this only encouraged attacking play. I lost six balls within the first quarter-mile and was forced to use a tennis ball in stretches . . .

Beyond a copse, a field of wheat opened out on the right. What looked like a swarm of vivid yellow insects hovered above it in places: oilseed rape, probably spread by the wind. In the early 1980s the European Community (as it was then called) decided we needed plenty of vegetable oils – used for cooking and margarine – and subsidised its production. Twenty years ago you rarely saw a field of oilseed rape: now it is a fixture of the pastoral landscape. The plant is a modern-day triffid. It stands as tall as a man and is poised to take over the world. As I was on my travels, The Government revealed that 6,000 acres of genetically-modified (GM) oilseed rape was growing across Scotland, much of it right here in Aberdeenshire.

# PAR 10,000

A rogue batch of seed from Canada effectively scuppered the 2003 moratorium on the commercial growing of GM crops. Having taken six weeks to mention this (during which time half of the seed in Scotland was sown) Agriculture Minister Nick Brown then urged farmers to destroy the crops since they couldn't legally be sold in the UK. There would be no compensation, he said, only payment for 'set-aside'. One Aberdeenshire farmer, who stood to lose 20 acres, summed up the mood when he told the media: 'We are having to go through hoops to comply with regulations, yet we are sold this duff seed. All these seeds were supposed to be imported into the country under strict supervision.'

The North-east is the centre for Scotland's GM crop trials. Some of the work is being carried out at the Scottish College of Agriculture, near Aberdeen, in plots no bigger than a bed. Women's tights are used to keep GM seeds together below ground, the fine mesh allowing soil organisms and moisture to pass through. The scientists involved pride themselves on offering impartial analysis about the impact of GM crops on the environment. The hosiery fetish is part of good scientific practice. It's the rubber stopper in the genie bottle.

The real worry centres on the field trials taking place at private farms throughout Scotland, most of which are in Aberdeenshire. At the start of 2000, six acres of GM oilseed rape and six acres of control plant were sown by Shirley Harrison who lives near Oldmeldrum. The plant was modified to shrug off a herbicide; the trial is studying the crop's impact on wildlife and insects.

She insists she isn't taking part for the cash (a pittance, apparently) but for the long-term good of the human race. Mrs Harrison, who spent 20 years in Africa, wants to grow crops that might one day yield new drugs and feed the world's starving. But Harrison is no quixotic fool. She believes farming shouldn't be 'restricted to using the same basic tools as we had 1,000 years ago' and was thinking as a businesswoman when she told the *Sunday Times*:

> Farming in Africa didn't prepare me for the agricultural subsidies which are given to growers in this country. But I do know they will end sooner rather than later and this whole industry will be unable to compete with cheaper output from other nations.

There are fears GM crops will cross-pollinate with wild plants to create a rampant 'super-weed'; you can't wrap a few acres of mature crop in hosiery. However, crops are usually modified to resist only one herbicide, not everything in the farmer's chemical arsenal, so any hybrid would be 'super' in a very limited sense. There's more chance the pollen will contaminate unmodified rape. A report by the Scottish Crops Institute for the Department of Environment warned this was 'inevitable under current agricultural practice' and predicted these seeds would germinate and thrive.

On top of this, farmers may saturate the land with the herbicide any crop is modified to resist – often produced by the company selling the GM seeds – wiping out all other plant life along with the insects and wildlife it sustains.

Just across the road from the Scottish Agricultural College is the Rowett Institute, former base of Dr Arpad Pusztai, the scientist who put GM food on the political agenda in 1998. His research appeared to show that rats fed GM potatoes suffered both damage to their immune systems and stunted growth. He didn't claim GM foods were unsafe, only that more research was needed.

Genes tell a cell to build proteins which form the specific characteristics of a plant or animal – the colour of its fur, or its resistance to disease. Scientists can tweak genes and alter existing characteristics. They can also introduce foreign genes. The gene that allows an arctic fish to withstand cold temperatures, for example, can be spliced into tomatoes, making them frost-resistant. However, genetic changes can also lead to the production of toxins within an organism, so tests are carried out for those harmful to humans. Dr Pusztai's great worry is that a new poison may be formed – a legitimate concern you would have thought. I mean, you don't run away from a bear because it looks like a bear. You run away because it looks dangerous.

The biotechnology companies were furious about Dr Pusztai's misgivings and the Government called for an investigation. The Royal Society dismissed Pusztai's work as meaningless, but then they were presented with the Rowett's analysis of the experiments rather than the raw data, he claims.

I've met Dr Pusztai twice – before and after this placid, self-effacing Hungarian became an unlikely champion of free speech. We sat in his lounge while his wife prepared dinner from fresh, organic ingredients, reflecting on the two-minute television appearance that had turned his life upside-down. His concerns weren't new, but by the summer of 1998 the world was all ears. Unfortunately, supermarket shelves were already heaving with GM foods. Dr Pusztai lost his job after 36 years. His health has since suffered but he wants answers not revenge.

'Instead of doing experiments with rats in the laboratory, there is one gigantic experiment with us as the guinea pigs,' he said.

I was forced to enter a wheat field when I found my path blocked by a tank-sized pile of manure. (Supporters of GM technology have pointed out that organically-grown food isn't entirely safe, highlighting the inherent risks of spreading hundreds of tons of cow excrement all over the countryside.) I followed a single-track road to Lethenty (some houses, a garage, a furniture studio), putting with the tennis ball, which absorbed the bumps much better than a golf ball. I gave way to a surprised learner driver who had been all set to pull over to the side of the road.

My 100th shot took me past a fold of pedigree Highland cattle. A few of these cartoonish beasts were grazing outside. They should really instil terror: prehistoric coat, no eyes, horns wide enough to skewer a chorus-line – but they have somehow acquired a docile, cuddly image. Some children probably think there's two people inside, one operating the horns, the other the swishing tail. They look too decorative to eat.

Back in the fields I found myself staring at three sack-sized boulders which lay against each other. They were contained within a small, square fence of uncut grass, and described on the map as 'Standing Stones'. 'Slouching Stones' would have been more apposite.

There are around 600 sites like this in the North-east, some of them 5,000 years old. The place contains the world's largest configuration of prehistoric and early-historic stones. Our ancestors weren't especially cookie; the area was already well settled by the early Bronze Age. Most stones stand on private ground and are protected by the Scottish Executive. Some circles (the recumbent stones, for example) are unique to the North-east and are thought to be linked to the phases of the moon.

The stones have long been associated with Pagan worship and you sometimes find wax and petals and other ritualistic paraphernalia lying around them. The rites are intended to create harmony between nature's cycles and our own. Paganism is now an offical religion in Britain and has an estimated 12,000 followers. According to the Pagan Federation, Paganism celebrates: 'the sanctity of nature, recognising the divine in all things, the vast, unknowable spirit that runs through the universe, both seen and unseen'. It respects all religions, doesn't proselytize, and seems to infuriate orthodox religions in the same way that very nice Liberal-Democrats madden Labour and the Conservatives.

According to rule 1-4/10 of the United States Golf Association's regulations (approved by the Royal and Ancient), a ball lying near a rattlesnake or a bees' nest constitutes a 'dangerous situation' and relief should be granted. From the far end of the field a herd of black cows came charging at me. Given that a cow can be as deadly as a grizzly bear, I thought it not unreasonable to take a drop on the adjacent road.

Putting was becoming a bore so I tried using a five wood off the tarmac. The tennis ball flew into ditch canopied by bushes – becoming yet another casualty of my impatience.

The monument to the Battle of Harlaw stands at the roadside like a giant peppermill, as high as a house, its grey and pink granite speckled with yellow lichen. In 1411, Donald, Lord of the Isles went on the rampage while Scotland's young king in waiting, James I, matured in England's finest jails. His army of 10,000 had camped overnight short of Aberdeen and was surprised by a smaller outfit assembled by Alexander Forbes, Earl of Mar. This was an almighty scrap between Highlanders and Lowlanders, the latter drawn from Aberdeenshire, Kincardineshire, Angus, and the burgh of Aberdeen whose provost Robert Davidson fell – and to whose memory the city erected this monument.

In an early act of spin-doctoring both sides claimed victory after slinking away at nightfall. Historians reckon the battle put a stop to the spread of Gaelic; all those soft elongated vowels were repelled that day. It became known as 'red Harlaw' because of its bloodiness and is commemorated in a chunky Doric ballad which concludes:

> And sic a weary burying
> The like ye never saw
> As there was the Sunday after that
> On the muirs by Harlaw
>
> And gin Heilan' lasses speer at you
> For them that gaed awa'
> Ye tell them plain and plain enough
> They're sleeping at Harlaw

I turned left into another matrix of fields and dropped towards the A96, the main Aberdeen–Inverness road. A sliced five-wood dropped in front of a house. The farmer, who hadn't seen the ball landing, stood by the fence with an elderly Labrador that was hunting for rabbits. He looked like an archetypal North-east farmer – ruddy cheeks, leathery neck, the splayed, fat-fingered hands of a mole.

Here was a man who made Kenny Dalglish sound like Ruby Wax. He wasn't unfriendly I guess, just taciturn. When you're standing in a somebody's field with a bag of golf clubs, miles from the nearest course, you expect them to initiate the conversation, but North-east folk are adept at containing their curiosity. If I'd been dressed as a Teletubby he wouldn't have flinched. The onus is on you to ask the questions.

'Is it just crops you have?'

'Crops and cattle . . .'

'Are the hares a pest?'

'Just the rabbits.'

'Somebody was saying you've to leave land set-aside.'

'Aye . . .'

'What's the soil?'

'That's for set-aside.'

'It must be frustrating, not being able to grow crops?'

'No, not really.'

You might think nothing could break a man of such stolidity, but you'd be wrong. Two years ago I sat round a coal fire on a December afternoon with some farmers. Their proud forbearance had hardened into abject fatalism. They spoke of tears and broken hearts. It was like the *Ricki Lake Show* live from Auchnagatt. One man admitted to being on anti-depressants after his wife had dragged him to the doctors 'by the scruff of the neck'. They'd each lost around £50,000 after the European Union's worldwide ban on the export of British beef on 20 March 1996.

Next the Government outlawed T-bone steaks on the 15 million-to-one chance someone might contract the human form of BSE. 'Do you ban a sweetie because a child might choke on it?' asked one of the farmers with the same angry incredulity Magnus Sinclair had displayed.

A track on the other side of the A96 carried rainwater off a hill, sluicing it over my shoes. When the ball ricocheted off a rock into a field, I remained there among the barley shoots and hit several good irons, long and straight, dropping them squarely between tractor marks. The footpath I expected to see on my left was long overgrown, annexed by raspberry bushes, broom and mature sycamore trees. It must have been years since anyone had used it; perhaps those retreating from the Battle of Harlaw came this way.

Bennachie draws you on. Although it's only 1,800 feet, not even a mountain, it always contrives to look higher than it is because of its 'Walnut Whip' profile. The hill is visible from every quarter of the North-east except the west where the Grampian Mountains swell. It stands over the area like a beacon, like a breast you can suck on. When you see Bennachie you know you're home.

At the top of the second barley field a mobile phone mast reared up like a kebab skewer.

WARNING: RADIO FREQUENCY ENERGY

FOR YOUR OWN SAFETY YOU ARE ADVISED NOT TO PASS OR STAND WITHIN THE HAZARDOUS AREAS SHOWN IN RED. PERSONS FITTED WITH CARDIAC PACEMAKERS OR SIMILAR DEVICES ARE ADVISED TO AVOID ANTENNA.

The caution was printed on a small, A4-sized notice – pinned *within* the perimeter fence. Beneath these ominous words a stick-man could be seen fleeing the mast. To figure out where you shouldn't be standing, you first had to step right up to the mast, an interesting conundrum.

A golf ball was leading me into the darkest crannies of the countryside and I was happy to follow it – through dung heaps, firing ranges, fetid swamps, ghostly farms and now microwave radiation. If all that wasn't off-putting enough, a big cat is said to roam these parts.

The 'beast of Bennachie' is thought to secrete itself within dense woodland during the day and hunt at dusk. There are around 20 sightings every year in the North-east. In May 1999, a vet living in Alford (on the other side of the hill) suggested that panthers released from a private collection may have bred and established a colony. She said: 'They are definitely there and a lot of people have seen them, but a lot of people don't mention it.'

The Wild Animals Act of 1976 made it more difficult to run a zoo in your living room, and some big cats were probably let loose at this time. (In 1980 a Speyside farmer caught a puma with a box-trap.) However, the chances of these solitary animals meeting and reproducing would have been extremely rare.

The North-east's big cat *could* be an indigenous but as yet unidentified species, possibly a survivor from the Ice Age. This theory has been put forward by Diane Francis in several books. For years she maintained a black wildcat existed and eventually presented the Royal Museum in Edinburgh with a carcass as proof. As for the 'big cat', Diane, who based her studies in the North-east, described an animal familiar to many, one the size of an alsatian, black and very muscular, with pricked-up ears, a flat face and a long curling tail.

Every so often a sheep is found slaughtered in a field, gnawed to the bone, but this is almost certainly the work of a dog. A big cat kills neatly and quickly with a suffocating bite to the throat and will stash its prey in a ditch or a tree, sometimes covering it with dirt or leaves. A dog tears from underneath. Dr Hans Kruuk, a zoologist called to study the killings, felt impelled to point out that an ordinary cat can assume monstrous proportions when seen at distance – or in poor light, which would also explain why the animal is often simply described as 'black'. He knows how easy it is to be fooled too, having once mistaken a jackal for a lion on the Serengeti . . .

The 'beast of Bennachie' could also be a rottweiler. Six years ago a puppy went missing in the Garioch area. Get this – its tail hadn't been docked. Even Grampian Police, the most sober of forces, conceded that it was possible the dog had reverted to a wild state. If this is true it is probably quite a timid animal, thoroughly scared of the rambunctious humans who pass through forests, pogo-ing bikes and swinging golf clubs as they go.

By now it was a fine evening. The rain had gone, leaving a milky sky. From the hilltop, I could see fields of variegated barley spreading all the way to Oldmeldrum; the winter-sown crop pale golden-green, the spring-sown crop darker in hue. And between them, clinging to this corner of Scotland like giant 'Post-It' notes, lay the oilseed rape.

Descending towards the Chapel of Garioch I swapped a Pinnacle Gold for a plastic 'Winnie-the-Pooh' ball that could be driven over the deep grass. A well-hit five-wood sent it as far as a genuine golf ball under a nine-iron. On reaching the road I chased the same ball towards the village and past a primary school filled with sunlight and shadows, the day's lesson still there on the blackboard ('this is what happened when the red dye moved up the celery').

The ancient chapel is exactly where it should be – in the midst of the dead. Some gravestones are sunken and worn smooth by the rain, names faded above ground, bodies assimilated below. These could have been the graves of my forebears for all I knew. All those who had once cared were in the ground too.

Many people like their graveyards to be pretty, the connotation of permanence and order. Aberdeenshire Council didn't just shut public loos to save money; it has tried to reduce grass-cutting at cemeteries. The plan unravelled when a growth retardant was washed away in May's heavy rain. The grass and weeds flourished and public fury forced a U-turn of sorts. The grass at Garioch could now have passed as a fairway but a graveyard is no place to swing a golf club.

The map showed a path leading from the chapel to Pittodrie House Hotel, but this had become smothered by plants, reclaimed by the living, prehensile planet. So I putted along the road instead, towards the long rhododendron-lined driveway of the hotel where I would spend the night, finishing on 349.

**STROKES: 349     TOTAL: 1130     SCORE: -245**

## *Etiquette*

If a golfer decides to throw his club away in anger he should only do so when the players in front are out of range. If his playing partner also wants to launch his club down the course, the player whose ball is furthest from the pin has priority. Do not swear within earshot of golfers on other courses. When urinating on the course, avoid bunkers and water hazards. Players do not have to replace divots in a bunker but they should rake over their footsteps. Players should kick only immovable objects such as trees and tee bins. Players should wait until they are off the green before tearing up their scorecards.

# FIVE

# Echoes of Royal Tink Dee

**HOLE 5     DISTANCE: 7 MILES     PAR 438**

ALL GOLFERS fantasise about creating their own course. They will look wistfully at piece of land and picture it flowing towards a bowled or elevated green, imagining the tee box, some bunkers and the tall fluttering flag.

This reverie can happen anywhere – on the drive to work; while picnicking with the family in a park; during a romantic stroll across a links. Give us a pen and protractor and we'll use them as effectively as Jack Nicklaus (who has designed many courses). Only the opportunity and the wherewithal eludes us. In Texas they recently recreated Scotland's 18 best-loved holes, flying in whole sections of turf. The cost: just ten million pounds. Now that would be a grand way to spend a Lottery win.

At 13, I was the co-architect of 'Royal Tink Dee'. A friend called Derek Thom and I mapped out nine holes in the farmer's field near our homes in Peterculter, a village eight miles west of Aberdeen. We used cardboard boxes for the tees, held fast with rocks. The flags were made from an old sheet, the numbers rendered in felt pen. It wasn't exactly a championship course but it did offer a surpassing view of the River Dee.

Fifteen years on, the village leaders did the same thing further upstream, on land sold to the city council by a farmer and rented to the club in perpetuity for a pittance.

These thoughts returned as I surveyed the 2,000-acre Pittodrie estate. I visualised a par-three rising gently between files of beech trees, stopping just short of the hotel. (The 18th, obviously.) The owner, Theo Smith, plans to fashion a real golf course from the swooping, verdant grounds within two years. He estimates it will cost a couple of million pounds and plans to pay for it by building and selling 20 luxury houses – something local planning officials have objected to.

'They didn't have a problem with the course,' he explained, 'but with the housing and its proximity to Bennachie.' Undeterred, he has appealed to the Scottish Executive.

I'd be surprised if Mr Smith gets knocked back. The Scottish Executive is currently preparing a 'national golf strategy'. It is hoped that this will reboot international tourism, and the Scottish Tourist Board has been asked to ready its own masterplan for luring the Japanese and Americans to a golf course near you.

Some people might despair of the Government's enthusiasm for golf, especially when health and other public services remain chronically under-funded, but they should bear in mind that the game generates £100 million for our economy every year. As it is, one in twenty Scots play regularly on the country's 500 courses, 60 new ones having opened in the last decade.

At least Mr Smith doesn't have the Global Anti-Golf Movement on his case. That said, he doesn't plan to chop down trees, reshape and irrigate the land, steep it with fertilisers, herbicides and pesticides, and displace native peoples. At Pittodrie the raw topographical ingredients – fertile soil, mature trees, a degree of cleavage – are already there.

For that we must thank Robert the Bruce who made a gift of the estate to the Earls of Mar for their support at Bannockburn. The fortified house dates back to 1480. The practical antique furniture is for sleeping in and sitting on; the log fires are there to please frozen hands not the sentimental eye. The hotel's ancient fittings and fixtures survive alongside central heating and satellite television because they continue to perform a function. There's no ostentation here, and in this sense Pittodrie House is quintessentially of the North-east.

After dinner I banged out some Beatles songs on the drawing room's grand piano, accompanied by Jess, the woman who had served my meal. I played the chords; she played the melody.

'If you get a fine January you get a bad summer,' she warned, referring to the year's mild start. 'That's what my brother says – and he's a farmer.'

A path leads directly from the hotel to Bennachie, climbing several hundred yards in under a mile. I carried a single club, a seven-iron, and a small rucksack containing a banana, about a dozen golf balls, my Winnie-the-Pooh ball and one I'd bought especially for the hills – a bright orange football.

There had been no word from my Professor Spracklen about the development of a ball with a built-in transmitter. Maybe the problem lay with building a casing sufficiently robust. Maybe he thought I was an idiot. The Royal and Ancient sets out a technical specification for a golf ball in Appendix III of the rules. I expected the football to be too big to conform but was thrilled to discover that the 'diameter of the ball shall be not less than 1.680 inches'. Think about it. *There's no need to outlaw a ball that won't fit in the hole.*

As far as I could discern the football had not been 'designed, manufactured or modified to have properties which differ from those of a spherically symmetrical ball' (stipulation number three). Not having a 'measuring apparatus approved by the Royal and Ancient' I obviously couldn't be sure the football didn't exceed the limits for the 'Initial Velocity and Overall Distance Standard', but it left the club with less alacrity than a Titleist and the 'combined carry and roll' was equally adrift.

Its one infringement was its weight. At five and a half ounces the football was more than three times the stipulated maximum. So why use it? Because I believe the weight restriction is there to limit density, and provides a simple way of doing so when all golf balls are manufactured to be approximately the same size – near the minimum diameter. A more compact ball will cleave the air better, conferring an advantage. A *balloon*-like football, therefore, was well within the spirit of the rules.

I struck it as I would a Titleist. When I connected it felt similarly meaty and let out a shimmying sound that made passers-by jump. The big ball was a cinch to control too. I used to think 'fade' was a euphemism for 'slice' but by placing the right foot ahead of the left I could swerve the ball with more panache than David Beckham, even bending it between pine trees.

As I gained height, regimented forest pines gave way to rowan trees and languid, soft-needled spruces, growing loosely on Bennachie's slope. Skylarks fluttered above, their fruity voices carrying like Morse code across the hillside, announcing the arrival of summer. The other dominant sound was a 12-bore shotgun firing in the grounds of Pittodrie. The hotel here will teach you clay-pigeon shooting, archery, fly-fishing; how to kill your enemy or catch your supper. I'd ask Theo Smith if he viewed golf as a frivolous game in comparison and he solemnly replied: 'No, I don't think so.' He used to be a member of Duff House Royal but, like many, gave up golf because of work commitments. 'I might play again,' he conceded, 'if there was course on the doorstep.'

It was a humid Sunday, the clouds gauze-like. Halfway up I stopped to laze in the heather. Within half an hour a dozen people passed on their way to the top. A mother with three youngsters and a dog, trudging along in big boots; a man with a huge tobacco-stained beard and a golf umbrella; four teenagers in *South Park* T-shirts – as motley a collection as you would find in a shopping centre.

'I hope you make it to the top,' said a woman, clocking my club as she bounced back down the hill, her face the colour of my football. The most inquisitive walker was a man of 78. Bennachie was the only hill he bothered with.

'Last year I was up three times,' he said proudly. 'This is my first time this year.'

He told me he had worked as a gardener in Aberdeen until he was 75. The hill was much busier now than 20 years ago, he said, but that didn't matter. 'I saw a lassie on a horse two years ago. I said to her, my god, lass, if that horse trips it will fall over its head . . . One year there was a band on top, folk with fiddles and pipes . . .' And now he would tell people he had met a man golfing his way across Scotland with a bright orange football. They would probably think him demented.

'My god I love it up here,' he said before moving off. 'It's just terrific.' It was only then that I noticed his dress – polo shirt, light anorak, slacks, ordinary shoes. If you'd told him about breathable waterproof fabrics he would have probably asked what was wrong with his skin.

He was right about Bennachie. It is everything a hill should be. It combines forest, moor and a rocky tor within a modest compass, and affords a perfect panorama of the North-east – across farmland, all the way to the coast and the granite-coloured North Sea beyond. It is very much a walker's hill; mountain bikes have little advantage here. The most interesting peak, 'Mither Tap', isn't the highest, an important discovery for the many youngsters who clamber over its slopes at weekends.

Bennachie is also steeped in history. Scotland's first recorded battle – 'Mons Graupius' – is thought to have taken place here in AD 84 when the Romans defeated a Celtic army which, unlike the rest of Britain, took exception to being invaded. The most significant thing the Romans ever gave northern Scotland wasn't the aqueduct or central heating but a sense of unity: they galvanised the diffident Celtic tribes into a band of irascible Picts. There's an ancient fort on Mither Tap, slung around the tor like two hoops, the bottom wall 15 feet thick. The core rocks are fused like molten glass. Archaeologists can make 'vitrification' sound like some dazzling building technique, but the chances are that this resulted from a spot of celebratory arson.

One hundred and nineteen shots had taken me to the point where you branch west to the highest top. The heather was short and crispy and I played the ball where it lay, leaving the path altogether. A grouse, disturbed by this wobbling fiery orb, sat up and strutted around in circles. That's the trouble with seeing wildlife on the hill – you've often got to flush it out. I was surprised this bird didn't fly off. It may have had chicks (I've seen a ptarmigan drop her wing, feigning injury in an attempt to lead walkers away from her brood), so I kept clear.

Oxen Craig here provides a marvelous view. On a cloudless day you can see the hills of Caithness, 129 miles to the north. The Cairngorms, still stained with snow, straddled the horizon some 70 miles away – the halfway point in my trip.

Bennachie, then, is the perfect antidote to Munro-bagging. (For those who don't know, any Scottish hill over 3,000 feet is called a 'Munro' after the man who first jotted down their names. Anything under this height is usually called 'a waste of time' by the baggers.) Many Munro-baggers therefore would give Bennachie a miss. Yet the view from one Munro is often exactly the same as another: all you see is the inside of a cloud. You know the view from the top isn't going to be any better than that from the ridge, but on you stagger through the mist, playing to some unseen audience. It makes about as much sense as your first kiss.

For many Munro-baggers, hillwalking is something better enjoyed in retrospect, ideally in front of a log fire with a pint of beer in their hand.

Typically, they start out trying to 'conquer' mountains; a quick fondling of the cairn and they're onto the next one. As they get older they become more respectful and describe hillwalking as a gratifyingly 'humbling' experience. Personally I don't need to feel like an ant to get excited about life; I've always found the fact that I was born something to marvel at. To a large extent our current aesthetic appreciation of wild places is culturally conditioned and entirely reactionary. Two hundred years ago Dr Samuel Johnson found our mountains uniformly terrifying and god-forsaken. They were, after all, the work of a vast anarchic force, a sort of glacial sludge.

So why climb mountains? Someone once ventured 'because they're there' but then so are lamp-posts – and you rarely see men and women claiming those as their own. In truth, climbing lamp-posts isn't so different from climbing mountains. Both challenges are contrived; lamp-posts are just less credible things to scale at the weekend if you're over ten years old. There's no gold star for climbing Bennachie, no table to be ticked. People do it because it's *fun*. They enjoy the hill for what it is, in all its moods, and climb it with or without friends. I guess you should no more judge the quality of a hill by its height than a round of golf by the number of shots taken.

I descended towards the Gordon Way. The heather became deeper and I was now exposed to the southerly wind. The quivering football would sometimes hover high above, making me look like Patrick McGoohan in the television series, *The Prisoner*, as he tried to outrun those curious throbbing balloons which looked like some bastard offspring of a Space Hopper and a condom.

The path I picked up was flat and free of people. I decided to waste some golf balls clawing back shots. (I should perhaps mention here that I wasn't in the habit of adding two penalty strokes for a lost ball since technically the whole 'course' was already out of bounds. . .) But within half a mile the Gordon Way shrunk in size and assumed the characteristics of a dry stream bed, forcing a switch back to the Winnie-the-Pooh ball after 291 strokes.

Far below on my left, the River Don lay as flat as a canal. I was now dropping towards the Howe of Alford. I joined a vehicle track (more lost balls) and then a path running alongside a pine plantation. I looked backwards and saw a sign: WELCOME. BY AGREEMENT WITH THE OWNER YOU ARE WELCOME TO WALK IN THESE WOODLANDS. THESE WOODS ARE SPECIALLY MANAGED WITH THE SUPPORT OF THE FORESTRY AUTHORITY. FORESTRY COMMISSION.

So far it was proving remarkably easy to gad about the countryside. In nearly 30 miles I had seen only one 'keep out' sign and no threats about prosecuting trespassers. I was as unfettered as the two yellow-hammers I watched tumbling through the sky ahead.

The last half-mile was delightful going, across grass that could have passed for a fairway. A combination of walkers' boots and a flock of sheep had kept the field flattened and groomed.

Ruminants fuss like barbers over grass. Years ago I tried to hire a goat to deal with a jungly garden at a flat I was renting. The breeder became stroppy on the phone, stressing that his animals weren't 'mobile lawn-mowers'. So I bought some weed-killer instead and mixed it all into a watering can, thinking it would do the entire garden. After covering three feet the can ran dry. The concentration of the herbicide in the raked soil must have rivaled that of Agent Orange. A blackbird gobbled a worm and keeled over on the spot. I haven't done any serious gardening since.

The last few hundred yards of the field had been freshly-cut and raked. This was surely a golf course in the making. I started to picture bunkers, a green, a lagoon fed by the nearby burn.

Three small paintings hang in Pittodrie House: *The Drive*, *A Difficult Bunker* and *The Putting Green*. The players in these paintings are rakish and patrician and the young caddies are bowed like grouse-beaters. The series dates from the late nineteenth century when the game's popularity soared with the introduction of the gutta-percha ball – which had the big advantage of being round.

It was a links course (probably one on the east coast) where the game gestated, and which I was now leaving behind. The tee, the fairway and green look much the same, formed by scruffy grass and sandy soil. It could have been the hillside I had just come off – or Royal Tink Dee.

**STROKES: 432       TOTAL: 1562     SCORE: -251**

## *Clothing and Footwear*

The physical nature of golf demands something soft and baggy. T-shirts and shorts for summer; a tracksuit for winter. The prissy nature of many clubs demands something starchy and squared-off. Here, a collared shirt is a must. 'Smart-casual', they call it. It's only recently that caddies on the world tour have been given dispensation to wear shorts (tailored, of course). After years of debate, dying of heat exhaustion on the golf course was considered more unseemly than showing a bit of ankle. Many golfers also wear gloves – but only one. Shoes with fine metal spikes provide grip. Plastic studs are kinder on greens but don't sound half as good on gravel. It is possible to buy socks with golf motifs but they offer no practical advantage. They are just socks with golf motifs.

# SIX

# Somebody's Garden

**HOLE 6  DISTANCE 4.5 MILES  PAR: 281**

TWO HUNDRED and fifty-one under par sounds stupendous. But consider this: I'd done just 27 miles of a 160-mile trip. That's halfway down the fairway of the second hole of a regular course – no place to start getting cocky. These were the easy holes. I needed to build an advantage to carry into the big mountains in the west where the fairway would be narrow and the wind could be devastating. Breaking 10,000 still remained a formidable challenge.

The last thing I wanted to do was end up in the *Guinness Book of Records*. As I write, 3,000 people have just taken part in the 'world's largest official Mexican Wave' which stretched two miles across the South Downs. *Why?* Probably because it's easier to set a new record than break an existing one, given that Guinness will accept inane challenges of your own devising. When it comes to golf, Jack Nicklaus's 18 major tournament wins is something worth taking a pop at. Nils Lied's 'largest drive across ice' (2,640 yards in Antarctica), Arthur Lynskey's 'vertical' drive (two miles down a Colorado mountain face) and Lang Martin's 'vertical golf ball balancing' (seven, North Carolina, 1980, if you must know) however, are not.

There are shorter, more tractable routes across Scotland than the one I was following, and bolder ways to play which don't require you to defer to crops, traffic and people. I'd set the nominal par as a way of maintaining focus, nothing more.

Dr Richard Cox, the Edinburgh University sports psychologist who turned Paul Lawrie into a world-beater, describes golf as 'not a game in which anger, despair or frustration are easily dissipated . . . It can get to you.' Six years ago he advised Lawrie to appoint a personal trainer and a nutritionist, breathe deeply, and look upon any shot following a duff as a challenge. According to Dr Cox: 'The people who generally get the best out of themselves are the ones who leave no stone unturned.'

So, I had a new attitude (positive-thought, shading gently into delusion) – and a new bonnet.

Actor and stand-up comedian Robin Williams described golf as a game where men get to dress like pimps. A cap can certainly appear dandyish. Wearing it forces you to take your game seriously – to *perform* – because that's the only way onlookers will take you seriously. Sear the ball 300 yards off the tee and those queuing behind will forget what's on your head. Shank it into the bushes and they'll think, 'who's the dick in the bonnet?'

Hat on, lungs full of air, head full of lop-sided hope, I crossed the B992 into another shorn field. The Gordon Way goes north-west but I was heading south-west towards the village of Alford. Two six-irons and a nine carried me to the next field (where I had to play over a sheep carcass). I dropped into another field and again made short work of it, before playing a glorious six-iron down a curling farm track, flying it over a field and holding it up on the path, four feet from my imagined pin.

On the 20th shot it finally happened: the ball landed in cow shit.

The Dunlop punched through the dark brown crust and sat mired in a rich olive paste, like a cherry on a cake. I'd crawled under gorse to retrieve the ball, picked it out of burns, groped among nettles for it, but I was tempted to leave this one where it lay. However, the more you study cow ordure the less noisome and stomach-churning it becomes – and for a salient reason: it doesn't look or smell anything like your own. You can't possibly regard a cow as a 60-stone man with chronic diarrhoea. (Similarly, sheep droppings are too coarse and too dry to belong in a toilet bowl. They look like something you'd pour milk over in the morning.)

I make no apology if all this offends. Shit is a big part of the outdoor experience. Aberdeen University microbiologist Professor Hugh Pennington, a world expert on the potentially fatal and liver-rotting E.coli 0157, described this new bug as 'something of a North-east speciality'. He was kind enough to offer me some candid advice about avoiding infection:

> Without mincing words, the simplest way to explain how it gets about can be concisely expressed as: 'by turd to tongue'. The bug

lives naturally in the intestines of cattle and sheep. It doesn't cause them any harm. Only when we eat or drink their manure do we fall ill. It is not possible to tell whether a particular cow-pat has the bug in it except by complicated laboratory tests. You can't tell by looking. So common sense has to prevail. If your ball falls into one – forget it. Don't lick balls, wherever they have been. Wash your hands before eating. A burn will do for this. But think before drinking the water. The places to avoid are the ones with a feeble flow and with a sheepfold just upstream. A powerful flow coming off a grouse moor without sheep would be much safer – but bottled water (Scottish of course) would be the only really safe drink of the $H_2O$ variety!

By the time I struck my 50th shot I had traveled more than a mile – again well under par for the hole. I was now on a road and able to putt downhill, gravity stretching the shots in a poor imitation of Arthur Lynskey's ingenious 'free-fall driving technique'. In a nearby field, two farm vehicles circled side-by-side, one uplifting cut grass and spewing it into a container pulled by the other. Seagulls floated behind, strung out like white bunting.

'They're after the worms and the mice,' said the young farmhand. I assumed this was set-aside. 'No, it's silage,' he said.

Yet again I was struck by how little I knew about farming. I could tell you about cities, I could tell you about mountains, but I could tell you nothing about the great skelp of land lying between them. I knew more about rare alpine mosses than about wheat; more about pine martens than the animals whose milk I drank and flesh I ate and skins I wore.

I was bleeding again after trapping my finger between clubs. After my paranoia of the pig farm though, I'd vowed not to worry too much about flesh wounds and poisoning. I never had done as a kid, and half hoped my body had built up some resistance.

The field by the house had also been cropped so once again I could hit long and hard. Runtish wheat grew in the next field, thinly spread out among the dry, stony ground. The Winnie-the-Pooh ball ended up in a burn where it floated off into a nether world beneath arching nettle bushes and grass. Fortunately, there were patches of earth I could string shots between using a proper golf ball.

Giant daises grew in the next field. They don't sprout on a bough but emerge from within the stem itself, a metamorphosis so complete I failed to connect the young green plants with the dazzling white and yellow blooms they produce. These weeds are common in suburban gardens but they are usually hauled up long before they have a chance to reach their radiant maturity. Gardening is a kind of genocide. At Pittodrie House, delicate lilac flowers grow under the shade of beech trees. The tiny petals of this plant, 'wood sorrel', are actually white and the colour spreads like ink on blotting paper, dark red down the middle, whispy pink at the edges. I'll bet it too gets thrown on the compost heap when it shows up in suburban gardens.

At the field's end I found a hare carcass smeared across a dyke, smelling exactly as you or I might in that condition.

The barley ahead was too mature to cross. In a matter of weeks the cereal had grown six inches, enough to cloak the tracks left by the tractor. Farmers exploit every square foot of their soil and barley is sown right to the edge of the fields, but it tends to be less dense on the periphery, and there was space for me to squeeze a shot down the sides.

I'd taken 111 strokes to travel three and a half miles – my best golf yet.

There was a wood to my left, bunched tightly behind rusting iron railings. I tip-toed across boggy ground to reach the open gate, around which decades of pine needles had gathered like drifting snow. A short uphill path – blanketed by the compressed needles – led to a tall, narrow building. Trees cloistered around it and almost brushed it with their branches. The map said 'mausoleum'. (Dead sheep, dead hares – now dead people . . .) Granite blocks had avalanched on one side, leaving a sandy ulcer high on the wall; the windows were picked clean of what I presumed had once been stained glass. Inside the tomb, a slab bearing the legend 'James Forbes Leith 1828–75' had been dragged aside and a rock dropped through what looked like a coffin below. Something else got my attention too – the sound of struggling from beneath a huge window shutter that had fallen to the floor.

The planet is never still. As it warms, cools and warms again, wood, stone and metal contract and expand, sighing as they do so. Spend a night next to a field of cows and you will hear them breathing, brushing against wire, flicking their tails – myriad sounds to prick the ears. And then there's the puppetry of the wind, jiggling branches, making leaves scuttle over the ground like mice. This noise was something less subtle, though, a rat or a bird maybe. Something a bit *Scooby Doo*.

I don't believe in ghosts. I can't believe that a spirit would walk the earth as some watery version of its previous incarnation, as something which can be approximated by draping a sheet over your head. No, the flapping and scratching in the mausoleum was a very corporeal disturbance. It would stop for half a minute then start again. Though the high curving roof acted as an amplifier, the movement, I realised, was too vigorous to be that of a rat or bird. An empty Heinz Lunch Bowl, lying beside the dislodged slab, increased my discomfiture. A slumbering vagrant? A kidnap victim? After a few minutes the noise ceased completely.

Okay, so I was too craven to lift the shutter but I was bold enough to stay and read the inscriptions: REV W FORBES LEITH OF WHITEHAUGH, 1833–1911 AND HIS BELOVED WIFE, MARIANNE LOUISA HARVEY. HE GIVETH HIS BELOVED SLEEP.

Sadly, this once grand mausoleum, now desecrated and crumbling, seemed to represent not a celebration of someone's life but a failed attempt to deny death the last word.

Back in the sunlight I pitched along a path between silver birches, using puddles as imaginary pins. Just short of the village I stopped to speak to a farmer, hoping to cut across a field towards the bridge over the River Don.

'Are those standing stones?' I asked, pointing to some unusually tall boulders growing behind a barn.

'Yes.'

'Not something you can pull out?'

'They've been here much longer than us.'

He confirmed the field across the road was his, and I asked if I could play through it.

'That'll be okay,' he said. 'But you won't lose any balls, will you?

'Eh . . . '

'Because the machines won't take kindly to them.'

As potential oversights go, this didn't quite rank alongside the Millennium Bug, but it still left me reeling. I'd grown up hitting golf balls about a field and just hadn't considered they might get the better of a combine harvester. The fields of the North-east are littered with stones; golf courses run alongside agricultural land; when green-keepers cut the rough atop tractor-like mowers they don't first sift out golf balls.

Was this farmer seriously suggesting that my Slazenger could bring a £50,000 machine to a smoking halt? The consequences were unthinkable. I'd lost 14 balls on this hole alone and dozens between Foveran links and Alford. North-east farmers had survived the BSE crisis, the strong pound, cheap imports. Now perhaps their existence would finally grind to a halt because of some sloppy golf . . .

A field is much more than a garden – it is someone's living. In crossing the land I had become very conscious of this, and had tried not use the club as a scythe. A fence, too, is someone's work and should be negotiated with care. I wouldn't have dropped a sweetie wrapper in these fields but had neglected to regard a golf ball as litter.

I produced my tennis ball and played on with dampened enthusiasm, crossing the bridge and putting along the road into the village. Suppose the cows ate the balls and started collapsing with bunged-up guts, like the victims of some new bovine plague? Suppose a shred of golf ball wound up in somebody's breakfast cereal and they choked on it? Was I worrying unduly now – or had I been too cavalier at the outset?

Alford Golf Club lies to the left of the road leading into the village. Players strolled along in T-shirts, making me feel like a right bloody idiot. A sign at the course boundary said: WARNING TO PEDESTRIANS. BEWARE OF STRAY GOLF BALLS. I stepped over a short fence and stood on the eighth tee, looking out over the mown fairways and shaved greens and the equally dapper rough, its grass cut and conditioned like hair. The hole was called 'Dinna Hook' because of houses to the left of the fairway. Another sign said: DO NOT ENTER ADJACENT PROPERTY TO RETRIEVE GOLF BALLS. (No, just leave your balls to blow up someone's mower or stick in the throat of their pet dog . . .)

THE Vale Hotel bar is as dark and timeless as a casino. You sit around it as you would around a roulette table, drawn by the sweetly-coloured beer taps and the comforting, rhythmical sound of a pint glass filling. I met John McKenzie there, who had been out on the River Don that evening. Five years ago, it seems, the trout were keener to take a fly.

'You've got to use a spinner,' he said. 'They milk the salmon upstream and release a couple of million parr [young salmon] into the water at the same time. The parr eat all the flies; they scoff everything. You catch a trout and out pops a parr. They take one in the morning and just sit for the rest of the day. It's made them cannibals. We shouldn't be messing. We should leave the fish to their own devices.'

**STROKES: 158      TOTAL: 1720      SCORE -374**

# A Lesson

I fly the ball down the range. 'You'll never hit a decent shot,' says Hamish Love – a PGA-accredited coach – 'not like that anyway.' Within 30 minutes he has revolutionised my game, put 10 to 15 yards on a shot by getting me to close the club face on the ball rather than spooning it into the air. Breaking 90 should be easy. Three months later I whip a ball through the air – further this time, but he is still shaking his head. 'Unadventurous,' he says. He trains a video camera on me and juxtaposes the footage with some of Paul Lawrie in the same spot. Hamish has the relaxing intonation of a bingo-caller: 'Turn-your-shoulders . . . through-90-degrees.' If I can straighten my left arm, he assures me I will break 80. 'Great-coordination. . . great-follow-through.' (Seven-and-nine, seventy-nine . . .) Now I just need to try it with a ball.

## SEVEN

# Sheep Country

| HOLE 7 | DISTANCE: 6 MILES | PAR 375 |
| --- | --- | --- |

IN THE fourteenth century Okakura Kukuso produced the seminal *Book of Tea*. Here he described the tea-room as 'a mere shack' with its 'air of refined poverty' and spoke of the garden path 'breaking the connection with the outside world'. For me, 'tea-rooming' has always been a quasi-religious experience, or at the very least a verb in its own right. And a journey into the countryside, I think, is analogous to Okakura's trip along the garden path.

The greatest tea-room I ever visited was a mere shack. The Cairn-mon Earn stood at the top of 'Slug Road', which climbs from Deeside over into the Mearns. It had mis-matched crockery and cutlery, bought at auctions; a mannequin stood outside in a jauntily worn hat, modeling second-hand clothes; the roof was corrugated iron. My pals and I used to visit it on a Sunday afternoon after a boozy night out on the town. Our hangovers would dissipate there in a fug of hot tea and fresh-baking. This was our absolution. The tea-room eventually burned to the ground and so passed into legend.

The Cairn-mon Earn was the only tearoom to which we ever awarded five 'tea-pots'. I've done tea and scones at Reid's Palace in Madeira – a hotel so steeped in colonialism it offers its own blend of leaves – and even it doesn't compare. Fabulous scones, certainly, but a shade too formal, more like a library. Only four-and-half teapots, I'm afraid.

'Salad Days' on Alford's main street would probably have rated two. The fundamentals were right – table service, a good selection of cakes, an absence of tartan – but it lacked the surreal gentility of the best. In compiling his book *A Scottish Journey*, Edwin Muir visited the tea-houses of Edinburgh during the 1930s when women were debarred from pubs. He observed that women would 'languidly steep themselves until quite saturated', making the humble tea-house sound like an opium den. (More recently, Billy Connolly noted that the patrons resembled scones themselves, these squat elderly women with their white floury faces.)

Salad Days was quiet. The other customers included a teenage courting couple (he put a proprietary hand on her bum as they left) and an old woman in an Aberdeen FC toorie who seemed to be have been there all afternoon – possibly all week.

'So that's just a cup of tea then . . .?' said the waitress, gently but firmly urging her along. 'It was chilly in the morning but it seems to be warming up now. It's about time we were getting some blue skies. . .'

Replete with tea and cakes, I putted my way clear of the village along an unnamed road. A field of light grass and buttercups lay to the left. Two brown horses stood motionless at the far end. I chanced a tentative eight-iron along its length, determined not to loose any ball they might gag on. A cow was more of a commodity, destined for the slaughterhouse. These were someone's pets. It wouldn't have done to kill them.

A lane ran through Gallowhill farm, past machinery petrified by rust. The path was thick with bushes and I had to use the football, brushing past broom as I went. From a distance the yellow flowers had really shone. Up close they were less youthful, the petals having lost some of their lustre. It was now the first of July and the plants and trees seemed already limp and jaded. Summer was waning; nights were drawing in. On this overcast day the foliage appeared to be composed mainly of shadows.

I joined a road and attempted to match the Ordnance Survey map with the hills ahead, grappling with it as though trying to erect a small tent. Three elderly women stopped in a Renault Clio.

'Do you know where you are?' the driver asked.

'I'm not sure,' I replied. 'Do you?'

'No, we don't know where we are.'

'Do you want to know?'

'Oh no. We just like going for a tour.' And with that she drove off.

I followed the road for a bit before swinging right through a field of barley. The next contained short grass, stretched over a convex slope. Anything could have been waiting on the other side but by now I was wise to the clues on the ground. I bent to inspect some droppings – equine, fresh. As I reached the apex I saw two white horses feeding among ferns at the foot of the slope. One of them stopped eating and raised its head, eyeing me with curiosity, suspicion or anger – it was hard to tell which.

At first I was confident I could retrace my steps and reach the fence before being trampled, but as I watched, the trot became a canter then a gallop, and I asked myself a pressing question: could I really outrun a *horse*? A downhill green is always closer than it appears but this fractious-looking animal would soon be upon me. I bolted into some broom, clattering among the branches before bounding over the fence straight into a waist-high mix of thistles and nettles. At least I held onto my golf bag.

The next obstacle was the burn at the foot of the slope, which was wider than expected and steeply banked. I faced backtracking for half-a-mile unless I could cross it. A few hundred yards away a willow tree spanned the water, the branches tapering as they neared the far side. Edging along the boughs was like creeping towards the end of a seesaw. Pricked, stung, sweating and breathless, I dropped onto a boulder at the other side. I then reached a field of cut silage and reduced it to three five-irons. The two horses could be seen high up the hillside, nosing around the broom. Fifty penalty strokes seemed a fair trade for bypassing them.

The Grampian Transport Museum in Alford houses traction engines, a six-wheel-drive snow-plough and other impressively elephantine machinery. It also contains vehicles like the ill-fated Sinclair C5, a 1943 Buick tank destroyer used in the Balkans conflict, and a Maserati 250F, one of the greatest Formula One cars ever made. The curator, Mike Ward, campaigned to build a small oval track where he rolls out the exhibits on a regular basis, an eminently sensible way to run a transport museum. After all, you don't fill a zoo with stuffed animals.

The exhibit that got my attention though, was a video about roads. Admittedly a strip of sealed highway doesn't carry *quite* the excitement of a scarlet racing car or a machine that will put holes in a tank. It's hard to imagine, for example, that people collect and restore road surfaces and show them at concours events around the world ('now this piece of gravel was laid by General Wade himself. . .'). But without roads that Maserati would be no quicker than a cow.

The Romans built their own roads as they pushed north into Scotland 1,000 years ago. When they retreated they were kind enough to leave them behind but Scots were too busy killing each other to develop a national network. Decent roads were evidently a tool of oppression to them and it wasn't until the Jacobite rebellion that our rulers went to work, bridging rivers, linking towns and generally squaring the battle-lines. Tolls paid for improvements (a concept apparently too radical for today's motorist). One hundred years later trains threatened to make these same roads redundant, then cycling – 'the first national craze' according to the video here – restored enthusiasm.

I was expecting to make more use of roads and paths now that I was approaching sheep country. When you knock a golf ball towards a hill, you follow the instincts of the earliest civil engineers. You look for the easiest way over the ground. You don't concoct difficulties. That's called mountaineering.

The trees covering Langgadlie Hill were short and Christmassy, the forestry track broader than usual and carpeted with moss and grass. This, it turned out, was a veritable driving range.

An OS map may be the best in the world but the detail can only be superficial. It doesn't tell you what crops are growing in what fields, how deep the ditches are between them, and whether or not any animals grazing there are friendly or bellicose.

There was no guidebook I could refer to, nor would I have wanted to. As an adventure this didn't quite rank alongside those of Marco Polo or Captain Cook, but my heart did quicken every time I set forth, even if it was just along a country lane. I had to improvise everything from the shots I played to the mitigation I offered disapproving strangers. As such, the holes were proving joyously consuming.

It took 40 shots to reach the top of Langgadlie Hill. During my descent some sheep took exception to the football. They accelerated across the hillside, moving as one, as though funnelling towards an imaginary emergency exit. Of course the technical phrase for this is 'sheep *worrying*'. From below the farmer would see only panic, a fluttering white flag. I climbed higher among the gorse, outflanked the animals and drove the sheep back on themselves. The flock imploded and dispersed, creating an illusion of calm again.

The foot of the Langgadlie Hill was quagmire. Cows had punctured and churned the earth where I left barely a footprint. The museum video had explained that ruts created by cattle had for many years made the passage of wheeled carriages impossible in the North-east. The drovers used to fit their animals with metal hooves for the long journey south to market. Judging from these pot-holes, snow-shoes would have made a better choice.

As I'd already been told, '*A coo will tak' yer life*'.

The Health and Safety Executive (HSE) had just revealed that eight people were killed on farms in Scotland in 1999. (Or at least that was the number reported to the organisation; the real figure is thought to be higher.)

Different ways to die on the farm – falling through a roof; being crushed by a wind-blown tree while sawing it up; being crushed by a tractor overturning on a slope made slippery by evening dew; perishing in a barn fire. The other four fatalities this year involved animals, three of which 'were cows attacking workers who were checking on, or working with calves'. To give you a flavour of the HSE findings:

> Employee – 58 years – died from crush injuries to the chest after being trampled by a cow. He was among four workers who were de-horning calves. The calves had been separated from the cows which were in an enclosure in the same building. The calves were being handled in a cattle crush. As he returned one of the calves to the cows, its mother pushed the gate open and

trampled him. The other workers were able to restrain the cow but he died in hospital from his injuries.

Another death involved a ram which bolted and struck a farm worker on the leg. The man died in hospital two weeks later from a deep-vein thrombosis. David Mattey, the HSE's Chief Inspector of Agriculture said: 'Livestock handling remains an activity where particular skill and understanding is critical in anticipating behaviour and avoiding injury.'

The public, too, regularly die under the hooves of cattle. Section 44 of *The Countryside (Scotland) Act 1967* bans certain breeds of bull from being kept in a field crossed by a right of way. However, there are no specific prohibitions on other cattle and the law doesn't apply to moorland. When it comes to staying safe, the HSE offers this advice:

> All large animals are potentially dangerous. Most farmers try to ensure that the cattle they own or breed from are of a normally quiet temperament. However, when under stress (e.g. because of the weather, illness, unusual disturbance) or when maternal instincts are aroused, even normally placid cattle can become aggressive. Even gentle knocks from cattle can result in people being injured. All breeds should be treated with respect.

Anyone swinging a golf club near a cow simply deserves to be stamped into the ground. The thrust of the HSE's work is rightly to protect farmers and their employees. To this end it has produced a video on livestock handling – one of a whole series of dubiously titled offerings including *Don't Fall for It* (safety on farm roofs), *Fatal Traction* (farm transport safety), *Rash Decisions* (occupational dermatitis) and *Matter of Life and Breath* (occupational asthma).

One called *No Second Chances* uses reconstructions and interviews with accident victims to 'point out important safety advice for anyone who is working with farm machines . . . particularly maintaining or unblocking them'.

I find it hard to picture the average farmer settling down in front of the TV to watch *No Second Chances* (£14.85 to rent, £38.50 to buy), with an Indian takeaway on a Friday night, but that's not to decry the quality of the video. It won a Gold Medal at the New York Film Festival and

Grand Prize at the European Film Festival held in Edinburgh, which must make it infinitely more successful than just about every British film funded by the national lottery . . .

| STROKES: 362 | TOTAL: 2082 | SCORE -387 |

## *Practice*

The practice area is somewhere good golfers go to show off. Poorer golfers tend to feel intimidated and immediately resort to a swing they feel comfortable with. (That is, the one they have gone there to correct.) Consequently, a trip to the practice area can reinforce bad habits. You could try playing alone at night with a head-torch, but the degree of accuracy required can be forbidding. Alternatively, there's the custom-built driving range. There's usually a charge but the plastic tee mats are designed to flatter your play; taking divots is impossible. Hence the oft-heard lament: 'I was hitting the ball so well at the range . . .' And best of all, you're ensconced in a toilet-like booth where nobody can snigger at your swing.

# EIGHT

# Lost on Scar Hill

**HOLE 8     DISTANCE: 7 MILES     PAR 438**

I TRIED, I *really* tried, but you just can't play golf with a tall, heavy rucksack on your back. As you move your body in one direction the rucksack shifts in the other, wrecking the most compact, balanced golf swing. If you play right-handed the follow-through should leave your chest and hips facing the target; your weight on your left foot, right foot turned through 90 degrees, toe balancing on the ground; the figure-skater finish hinting at the kinaesthetic perfection of all that has gone before it. With a rucksack on your back however, you can end up on the ground, waving your legs in the air like an inverted beetle.

I didn't need to go to a practice range to find this out. A few swings in the back garden were enough to suggest back-packing and golf just don't mix. The 55 litre rucksack belted around my waist, with its alloy frame curving towards the base of my skull, cramped what little style I had.

This was one reason I wasn't trying to cross Scotland in a single attempt, as originally envisaged. (There were others – like getting time off work, keeping the blisters on my hands from bursting.) Instead I decided to tackle the holes at weekends and in the long, frisky summer evenings. When I moved further west, away from my home-base and into the mountains, I would have to consider swapping some of the clubs for a sleeping bag, but for the moment I was able to make it back to my own bed.

I parked my car at the entrance to Tillypronie estate – the finishing point of my hole eight – and got a lift from my aunt Sheila back to the southern side of Langgadlie Hill. The climb up Scar Hill started well. I called at a farmhouse to ask if I could play through their 75-acre set-up, more out of courtesy than anything. The woman who answered the door appeared apprehensive, so I promised to get past the farm track first before hitting any real balls. A young boy behind her reacted with the excitement you might reserve for greeting an alien.

The grass beyond was short and mossy, just right for the five-wood. After Fosbury-flopping over an electrified fence, I gained the summit of Scar Hill within 30 shots by following a vehicle track across short heather. The top was under cloud and splattered with seagull shit. Raucous birds wheeled incongruously overhead.

Already I was confused. As far as I could tell, this vehicle track wasn't shown on the four-year-old map. From where I was at the top of Scar Hill, the most prominent track ran west of a tiny lochan on the way to Craiglea Hill (where I was heading). However, the map showed the main track going east of the lochan. There was a track to the east marked but it seemed much fainter – not a track at all, more of a path. I continued towards Craiglea Hill, where I expected to pick up a series of paths curling west, but I could only really see vehicle tracks ahead (that is, two parallel lines in the heather). Everything made perfect sense eventually though when I remembered that an overgrown vehicle track is sometimes represented as a 'path' on OS maps.

Ordinarily, this wouldn't have been a problem but: (a) – the section of map I had photo-copied was dissolving in the drizzle; (b) – I hadn't bothered to take a compass; and (c) – the clouds felt like they were squashing my head. I tried following some of these tracks-cum-paths across the broad heathery hills but couldn't be sure I wasn't dipping into some glen that would bank north or coax me far off course. Cloud has an insidious effect on navigation; within half an hour I was thoroughly disorientated. I didn't know where I was or where I was going and had to declare myself lost.

I'm afraid I'm the kind of person who drives on third-party insurance and likes to walk that way too. Don't misunderstand me. I regretted not carrying a map and compass. They weren't going to save my life today, but they *would* have saved a lot of faffing about in the rain.

By turning to face the drizzle, wafted by a northerly breeze, I was able to work my way back to Scar Hill. After nearly two hours I returned to the farmhouse where I hoped to persuade the owner to call me a taxi. I had marked the position of my ball near Craiglea Hill and was resigned to coming back. Nobody answered the door. I knocked again. No reply – and yet I could hear voices just yards away through an open window. The occupants just didn't want to know. Maybe the golf bag had freaked them out. I slunk away, feeling like a pariah.

# PAR 10,000

The knock-back was a spur not to return. At the farm entrance I jettisoned the golf bag and my jacket, stashing them in a wooden shed. The car was nine miles away by road. There were three hours of daylight left; I had taken to wearing trainers. Using the tennis ball I would putt and jog, putt and jog, putt and jog. Scar Hill would count as a rebound.

The road was perfect, the newly-cut grass verges channeling the ball forwards. If you want to observe Scotland's wildlife at close quarters, just take a walk along a country road. I saw pheasants, partridges, a thrush, a roe deer and innumerable rabbits. (Shame they were all squashed and rancid.) The only car to pass within the first four miles was a police Peugeot. I saw it coming, trapped the ball under my foot, and stood aside as they drove by without a glance.

The clubs, 'Maxfli Pro Specials', had stood up well so far to the rigours of playing in perpetual, sometimes abrasive, rough. Even the putter, the only sane club for a road, was perfectly serviceable, although the heel was already heavily scoured. Maybe I should have persuaded Callaway or some other manufacturer to provide me with a full set of clubs. I'd have been happy to pose for an advert, perhaps bestriding the Lairig Ghru: 'Scotland's finest fairway, the world's finest clubs . . . Ten thousand reasons to buy Callaway . . .'

At half-distance I stopped to ask a farmer the time. (No, I didn't have a watch either.)

'Quarter to seven,' he said.

'Ten to,' a woman shouted from inside the house.

My last two miles included the A97 which links Dinnet and Huntly.

Putting along a trunk road isn't something you do lightly. There are considerable risks, not just to yourself. Any driver rounding a corner to find a ball bouncing down the road is liable to take evasive action. I'd half expect a child to come chasing after it too. However, the traffic was light. Approximately five minutes was elapsing between passing cars. I decided to go for it.

You need good ears for this caper. I was reminded of watching rallying, and the way you hear a car's engine bellowing and chirping among the trees long before it heaves into view, brilliantly marked and very often airborne, trailing a fantail of gravel, like some fantastical beast out to hunt you down.

I took a full swing only on open stretches where I could run to the ball and snatch it up before a car came round a corner or over a brow. I more or less walked it into the corners and treated apexes as a drop. A

Land-rover driver doubled back for a second look, but I kept the ball in my pocket. He could have been a keeper who had mistaken the putter for a rifle and me for a poacher.

The dog-leg wasn't too costly in terms of additional strokes. It pummeled my thighs, though. I was used to jogging, but not after golfing up and down a hill.

**STROKES: 380     TOTAL: 2462     SCORE: -445**

# Joining a Club

A good golf-club is like a dog pack – you must wait for the older members to die off before you can be a part of it. This can take decades. As a rule of thumb, if the average age of the members exceeds the course par it's worth putting your name down. If you find an established club that will accept you in under a year, don't get too excited. You'll probably find it's packing people in. Tee-times will be staggered by just seconds; a round will take days. That's if you can book a slot in the first place, what with the monthly medals, the junior competitions, boozy corporate outings and the paying public arriving in droves at the weekends.

# NINE

# Among the Grouse

**HOLE 9**   **DISTANCE: 16 MILES**   **PAR: 1000**

IN THE EARLY part of the year grouse are encouraged to make their homes on Deeside estates. Old heather provides shelter for nesting and the young heather – the shoots rising from burned moorland – is a source of food. The junket is brought to an end on 12 August; the fatted birds along with it.

It's a tough life being a grouse, but even tougher if there's more of you about competing for food. Keepers kill grouse to save them dying from starvation, the cold temperatures and disease. Seriously, that's what they tell you. They could leave this to the fox, but the fox isn't willing to pay hundreds of pounds a day for the privilege of killing grouse. Shooters, on the other hand, will. For this reason, game-keepers spend much of their year killing foxes.

That task could soon be made much harder, as keeper Sandy McConnachie explained. We got chatting as I was putting past his home which sits below Morven. Sandy works on the Tillypronie estate. He has the quietly assured, decorous manner of many a keeper, but admits to being fretful about moves in the Scottish Parliament to ban any form of hunting with dogs.

'A fox will go into rocks and we've got to use terriers to chase them out,' he said. 'You want a dog to bark and create a disturbance, but you don't breed it to be aggressive. If it ends up getting mauled it's out of action for two or three months. And then you've vet's bills.'

And if the fox went unchecked? 'It would cause an awful devastation. We'd have no stock left.' He sounded as disenfranchised as the farmers I had spoken to.

I'd hoped to head south from Sandy's house but the way forward was blocked by cattle and mature barley – the last crops I expected to see this side of the Cairngorms. I continued west into Balronald wood where play was awkward. My golf ball would ricochet among the pine branches, dropping back onto the path or sliding silently from view among the ferns. This wasn't golf – this was pin-ball. I stuck with the football but it wasn't at its best here. It took 138 shots to clear a mile of wood.

A dyke marked the forest edge. It was covered with lichen, grown like a coat to protect it from the wind. On the other side, heather stretched across the eastern slope of Morven, as uniform as sand and just as enervating to walk through. Swinging a club was awkward, especially on steeper sections. I often had to carry the ball up or down the hillside to find a lie I could play from without falling backwards. The mix of heather, blaeberry and fern left me foundering, the accursed golf bag swinging back and forth like an over-sized arrow quiver. Within half a mile I was sweating like cheddar and smelling no sweeter.

Two grouse rose from my feet and fell away across the slope, yacking as they went. They had perhaps a month or two to live, before shooters raked these moors and brought them tumbling from the sky in their hundreds.

I spent a couple of seasons working as a ghillie on a Deeside estate and remember vividly the sights and smells of grouse-shooting: a puff of down floating across the heather like dandelion seed; the smokey tang of gun-powder wafting behind it; a dog bounding after the bird, jinked right and left by a whistle as shrill as an oyster catcher's call; the grouse as floppy as a glove puppet, utterly forlorn, a drop of warm, syrupy blood hanging from its beak.

Only half the birds were killed outright. I had to wring the necks of the rest. Sometimes the head would come away in my clumsy hand. You could tell if it was young bird, another ghillie explained, if its soft skull burst under your thumb. An old grouse was any bird that had lived twelve months or more.

Many estates don't start shooting until September to conserve stocks. Grouse populations crashed dramatically during the 1970s and haven't really recovered. In the last decade the bag in Scotland has fallen from around 200,000 birds a year to one third of that. Everything from parasites to global warming has been blamed. As revenues have dropped, the cost of under-writing losses has risen to ten million pounds. The League Against Cruel Sports believes grouse shooting should be 'put out of its misery' and is encouraging landowners to seek grants to re-cover their moors with Caledonian pine, of which currently only a fraction remains.

Shooting, however, is more than a tradition: it is an instinct. Those involved are quick to defend both the practice and its economics. A few years ago one Deeside landowner told me: 'We're not asking for a subsidy. We're asking people to understand that we need income to maintain the land. We shouldn't denigrate a heather moorland just because it's man-made.'

Another 250 strokes brought me west towards the top of Coinlach Burn where the going was much better over the grass and short heather. A north wind bent around Morven and got behind the ball, allowing me to cover a mile in just 44 shots using a five-wood. Jacuzzi-sized peat hags were the only hazard. One contained the putrefying carcass of a ram, a lone horn curling above the black-green ooze.

The panorama here took in the conical Mount Keen, Lochnagar (its cliffs glistening with melt-water) and Ben A'an, more plateau than peak. If Deeside's pudding-like mountains lack drama, the skies often make up for it. The clouds which ball on these mountains dwarf them. It is easy to fantasise about climbing the towering, billowing shapes, rising white and sheer like the Himalayas, throwing out shadows the size of a village.

I was now facing the wind, which sent my big orange football spinning overhead. The grass and juniper bushes claimed 18 golf balls before I could again use the football. Dropping towards Glen Gairn, I left the track to cut across the heather. Three hillwalkers I had seen coming off Morven were getting into a car below. They gawked up at me, pulled away, halted, gawked again, drove a few hundred yards, then halted again. As I drew closer they kept moving on in the frustrating way some animals do when you try to steal upon them.

The vehicle track was too stony for a golf ball so I stuck with the football, having forgotten to replace the last of the tennis balls in my bag. Two men sat outside Lary farm, shearing sheep with scissors in the late-afternoon sunshine. They weren't in the mood for talking, and I wasn't in the mood to cajole them.

A Land-rover and an Audi estate rolled up to Morven Lodge, and a girl got out to open the gate. That's a ghillie's job. When I was a ghillie I had once found myself hanging off the back of a packed Land-rover as we bumped our way towards a grouse moor. Scared my arms would give out, I had asked one of the shooters following behind if I could ride in his Saab. One of the party got out at the next gate and laughed heartily as she waved me through. She thought my audacity was hilarious. (The keeper was less amused and very nearly sacked me.)

# AMONG THE GROUSE

I used my last golf ball crossing two empty fields with a six-iron. With my boots tied around my waist and using the putter as a staff, I waded through the sparkling River Gairn to reach the A939. I had taken more than five hours to cover nine miles and so I was relieved to hitch a lift within five minutes.

Eric Duncan, a retired serviceman, offered to take me down Deeside, saving a lengthy wait for the bus at Ballater. He had just climbed Morven for the first time since 1944. A local man, he proved to be engaging company, pointing out the house where he was born, woods where hazelnuts grew in abundance and much more besides.

'The wind was awful on Morven,' he said. 'There were three Germans there. One tried to take a picture but he couldn't stand up and had to kneel. I tried to speak to them but they didn't know much English.'

I wonder what they would have made of my orange football.

'Bloody dead . . . It's normally stowed-out at this time of year. There's some Germans about and some Dutch, but bloody few of them.'

The taxi driver was remarking on the quietness of the A93 and on the dearth of tourists. 'It's obvious what the problem is. The strong pound and the price of petrol. In Ballater it's only one pence a litre cheaper than in London, and in Strathdon it's six pence dearer . . . If you're a holiday creature you'll go abroad.'

I had parked my car at Balmoral and was returning to Glen Gairn.

'You go down to Glen Muick and you're lucky if you see one sheep now,' continued the driver. 'Twenty years ago there used to be five to ten thousand. Landowners want all the sheep off the hills. They don't want farmers as tenants because they've got to pay tax on the rent they get, but they don't pay anything on the shooting because there's no such thing as a "sporting tax" now.'

Only habit, he reckoned, kept the farmers clinging on.

'I was reading that in 1958 a ewe was worth a fiver,' he told me, 'that's more than they're worth now. Maybe they farmers have had it too good . . . Their sons won't stay. It's probably a blessing.'

The ten-mile journey cost me £12.

I set off through calf-deep heather, punting the football with a six-iron, the only club I was carrying. I'd picked up 50 golf balls for a fiver at a car-boot sale and had packed some of these into my deep jogger pockets (if only I could have stored them as fat). Fortunately, the wind was subdued and I quickly gained Creag na Creiche, crossing a moor where around 50 pines had been chopped down. The trees lay among the heather, their bleached branches poking up like parts of a rib-cage.

The next few miles were all above two thousand feet. The evening sun was still warm on my face; the view of mountains, forest and river the best yet, and the short, bouncy heather as user-friendly as a golf-mat.

Shot after shot I watched the ball land and sit up, fully 100 yards away. The exhilaration I felt at this point was like that of an obsessive inventor who finally gets his device to work. If anyone doubts it is possible to golf meaningfully on a mountain they should make for Creag na Creiche. Some people, I sensed, had dismissed me as a crank or a charlatan. There were certainly times when I felt like both, when the futility of the play mocked my ambition. Up here, however, I felt vindicated.

As I descended Gellaig Hill, gliding down towards Balmoral Castle, the heather grew thicker, though the path was wide and easy to hit. There were plenty of hares about but surprisingly few grouse and no red deer. I sent up a snipe, as I had done as ghillie. Back then, the shooters excitedly turned their guns on this small, fast, challenging target – calling, 'Snipe! Snipe!' – and I willed the bird to get away, which it did. It was an individual among a blur of plump brown grouse. When I'd jokingly asked the Saab driver if shooters got more points for a snipe he looked at me blankly.

The golf balls ran out just before the last hill and I resorted to the stroke-sapping football, doubly frustrating because short grass fields made up the last quarter-mile of this hole. After skirting a wood of pine and silver birch I reached the Knock Gallery, home to Alicia and Bruce Thomson. It showcases artwork from Scotland and Eastern Europe – paintings, etchings and jewellery made from Polish silver and forty million year old Baltic amber. Bruce's own sculptures include a life-size foal rising to its feet and Icarus diving from the sky, his straining limbs evinced by the crooked, tapering birch branches.

'I tell people they won't find any stags on crags here,' said Alicia, laughing.

Bruce's family has belonged to Crathie for more than 300 years; Alicia is Polish. They made their home here 20 years ago when the building was derelict and the surrounding ground barren. Carefully cultivated plants and hardy shrubs now thrive at 1,400 feet, making this one of the highest gardens in Britain – all without the help of Charlie Dimmock.

Their daughter, Sophie, offered me a glass of 'smooth and grassy'

Lochnagar malt whisky, a graduation present from the nearby distillery where she worked for six summers. Her main subject was environmental history.

'Before I went to university I was blinded by sentiment,' she said as we discussed hunting, dogs, foxes and politicians. 'Now I've got a feeling they're kind of interfering where they shouldn't be. I tend to come down on the side of the keepers. It's got to be done.'

I finished my drink, said goodbye and returned to the car. The view – Lochnagar's discreetly bared corries, tall gilded firs, a lion rampant rippling above Balmoral's granite tower – is one the Thomsons said they never tire of.

**STROKES: 1004     TOTAL: 3466     SCORE: -441**

## *The Golf Shop*

Wood covers in the shape of monkeys, giraffes, lions, elephants and fish. Covers for your irons. A cover for your covers. Tees for the winter – small flared cups to straddle the frozen earth. 'Unbreakable eyeglass cases' (pictured with a black golf-shoe weighing down on them). A re-usable scorecard with 18 tiny ratcheted wheels to display the strokes taken. A digital scorecard. A telescopic 'wire retriever' to scoop your ball from a burn. Bands to support your wrist. Bracelets to support your superstition. Gloves for dry conditions. Gloves for wet conditions. Gloves for changeable conditions. A water-bottle designed especially for golfers which contains, among other things, a 'handy divot tool'. A golf ball monogrammer. A putting practice-mat with a palm-sized bunker and lake either side of the hole. The 'complete' St Andrews gift set: ball, towel, marker, tees and pitch repairer. A fake St Andrews membership tag . . . Just don't get started.

# TEN

# Royal Deeside

**HOLE 10     DISTANCE: 7 MILES     PAR: 438**

PRINCE ANDREW couldn't make it. Balmoral has its own 18-hole golf course that can be glimpsed from South Deeside Road. I was hoping the Duke of York might be up for few holes, keen golfer that he is. Miss Charlotte Manley, OBE, Comptroller and Deputy Private Secretary to the Duke of York, wrote:

> The Duke of York has asked me to thank you for your letter of the 29th April in which you asked to play a few holes on the golf course at Balmoral. His Royal Highness appreciated your letter and sends you good wishes for your venture. However, His Royal Highness will be unable to join you at any stage during your 'golf match' across Scotland. For your information, the course at Balmoral is open to members only. I am sorry to be the bearer of disappointing news. The Duke of York has asked me to convey his good wishes.

I wrote again, asking if a less sovereign member of the club could be persuaded to act as chaperone, and also inquiring about how I might go about joining. Estate factor Peter J. Ord replied:

> I am sure that you are aware of two excellent golf courses at Braemar and Ballater. I think it is more appropriate that these should appear in a book about golf rather than the Balmoral course. The use of the Balmoral course is restricted to members who are either members of the Royal Household Golf Club, who work on Balmoral Estate, or who live in Crathie Parish and have a close association with the Estate. The course is maintained by

only one greenkeeper, and we try to restrict its use in order to keep wear and tear to a minimum, and to keep costs of maintenance firmly under control.

He seemed to have missed the point. Still, I didn't fancy sending another letter and finding myself under investigation by security forces. Sneaking on wasn't an option either. Taking turf would constitute vandalism and there was always the chance I would be wrestled to the ground by a plain-clothes detective – not what you want when you're putting.

It's quite a luxury, a private golf course. There's another in the North-east, on the 53,000 acre Dunecht estate which is owned by Charles Pearson, son of the late Lord Cowdray.

Like Balmoral, this course exists for estate workers, tenants and local people. The ranger is 80-year-old Alex Smart who still pitches and putts around the greens every day. Years ago, when 'the gentry' were staying, no-one could use the course until after 6 p.m. Alex always made sure he was first off the tee.

'The butler used to present the gentry with a few boxes of Silver King golf balls every day,' he recalled. 'The gentry didn't bother to look for them if they couldn't see them. Sometimes you'd find these brand new golf balls lying on the fairway . . .' Silver Kings are worth £100 today.

A few years ago Alex wrote a letter to the laird, one that provides an insight into the relationship between a major landowner and their employees:

> Yesterday sitting on the seat at the fourth tee, I got to remembering when the course was reconstructed to its present form. At this time, the Keepers reared ducks and I think your father didn't want any disturbance when the time came for them to be shot, so he gave the land across the road which was drained and seeded creating the layout as it today.
>
> When it was completed in 1936 it was decided, as Lord Cowdray and his party were in residence, to ask if they would officially open the new set-up by driving the first ball of the new fourth tee. Now, it was well known that golf was not his favourite sport, indeed the story has always persisted here that when your Father was recuperating from losing his arm in World War Two he remarked that at least he wouldn't have to play golf again!
>
> However to the delight of the Committee he agreed and a night was set for the occasion. At that time Mansion House

parties were large and there was quite a following as the party reached the tee. All the Committee were there and the heads of departments, including my Father who was a founder member when the club was set up after World War One.

I was 16 at the time and of course was not included, but I was determined to be there so sneaked up and found a nice vantage point.

I do not think the locals expected much from His Lordship especially when he was getting all sorts of advice from his friends. However, it was clear from his few practise swings that he had a fair idea of what he was doing. To the astonishment and delight of the locals his ball went long and straight, back then it was a marvelous shot.

They were golden days the thirties. When the War came a few years later nothing was to be the same again.

After the war people wanted more of everything, said Alex – including golf clubs. The size of sets doubled. 'People used to do fine with five,' he lamented.

Just short of Balmoral I came across a man hitting golf balls in a field across the road from his mother's house.

'There aren't many driving ranges around here,' he explained.

Ian Stewart-Grant was born into a farming family on Deeside 48 years ago. 'I started playing golf when I was eight or nine,' he said. 'I used to play at Balmoral with Jimmy Thow, the son of the gardener. I was awful cack-handed though.' As a boy he made a putting green on the front lawn and invited bed-and-breakfast boarders to play. 'I use it for chipping now.'

Ian manages a visitor centre in Perthshire. He was a lapsed golfer until a few years ago:

> I was self-employed as a sheep-shearer at the time. It was work, work, work. My wife Janet said I should take up a sport. I had a lesson with a professional who said I should try playing left-handed. That made all the difference. Now I can't get enough of golf. It's an obsession. Sometimes I take balls to work and practise there. Janet says I should be a professional by now.

Ian is a member of Whitemoss Golf Club which opened near Dunning in 1994. His playing partner is a minister. 'We're known as the eight-hour golfers because that's how long we take to complete a round. We take a piece out with us and stop for lunch.'

It was time to hit some balls.

Ian, a 19-handicapper, flexed his gloved right hand and walloped a five-wood towards the Dee. (The field was normally full of sheep but the farmer who rents it had taken the animals away to be sheared and dipped.)

'The grass disappears in autumn and mum collects the balls that get stuck in the tufts. I bought her one of these to save her bending down.' He held up a practice tube like the one I was carrying. 'Well, she is nearly 80.'

'I'm determined to master golf', he told me, 'maybe that's because I took it up again late in life. I enjoy taking on a scratch player and getting my teeth into a fella . . .'

Our talk turned to the peculiar difficulties of golfing in heather, prompting me to get the football out. Ian found that by playing off the back foot he too could control the swerve. He hit another wood.

'This is how it was when they started at St Andrews,' he said.

We continued to blat the football back and forth across the field, two 'bloody nutters' at play, oblivious to the world and our place in it. I'd known Ian barely ten minutes but our shared passion transcended the need for further talk. I could have been back on my parents' front lawn, a small boy aiming for the neighbour's hedge. Sometimes, Ian drives a ball from his mother's lawn into a nearby wood where he knows he will never see it again.

'I just love hitting the ball . . . and what better place than this?' he said, gesturing to all of Deeside.

'We've heard about you,' said the security guard flatly, eyes averted, hands behind his back, everything delivered as a statement of incontrovertible fact.

I was standing outside the entrance to Balmoral Castle, cap on, golf bag across my back, football hanging from it in a plastic supermarket bag. I wanted to pick up the Old Military Road that runs through the estate alongside the River Dee. This was the easiest way of reaching Braemar. That it happened to be the Queen's back garden was coincidental.

Like the Royals, my family used to holiday at Deeside. We'd take a caravan at Ballater and share the same pleasures as the Queen – walking by the Dee, imbibing the pine-scented air, climbing a small hill with a big view.

The local bakery here sold the best butteries I've tasted – saucer-sized, crispy on the outside, fluffy on the inside, with just a hint of salt. Like several shops it displayed the royal crest outside – the official seal of approval. The Queen, apparently, was in the habit of driving into the village to go shopping, although my dad never saw her in the queue when he collected the butteries.

The people of Deeside don't make a fuss of Mrs Windsor and I guess that suits her fine. Neither are they exploitative. The Balmoral household has rarely blabbed to the press. The world, for example, still waits to hear what videos the Royals rent to watch on long, rainy days stuck inside the castle. It must be an insular, almost quarantined life – sleeping in the bed where you may have been conceived, wandering the corridors like a ghost. I think of the Queen sitting in the servants' quarters, feeling strangely cheered by the framed photographs of their loved ones, by this unashamed attempt to make her home theirs.

If those in Ballater are indifferent about living next door to the world's most famous family, like all good neighbours they quickly close ranks. Years ago I met a fisherman at Loch Kinnord, further down Deeside, who said the best place for trout was 'Charlie's Loch' – a stocked loch next to Birkhall, the Queen Mother's holiday home on the Balmoral estate. When I casually asked about the loch in a local tackle-shop the owner denied such a loch even existed – although the trout I later hooked and returned seemed real enough.

The security guard was finally convinced I wouldn't break any castle windows.

'On you go,' he said, allowing me to join a stagger of Americans getting off a coach. I noted a sign inside the gate: VISITORS ARE ACCEPTED TO BALMORAL GROUNDS ON TERMS THAT NO LIABILITY IS ACCEPTED FOR ANY INJURY HOWEVER CAUSED.

That's me off the hook then, I thought – at least as far as killing any tourist goes.

Sixteen putts with the tennis ball brought me close to the baronial castle. It was built in 1855 for Queen Victoria. For the price of a couple of pints of beer you can wander the grounds where there's a wildlife exhibition, ornamental gardens and you can go pony trekking. As far as I could tell, only the 'Queen's Ballroom' in the castle is open to the public. One hundred yards before the entrance a sign warns, NO DOGS BEYOND THIS POINT. At the doorway the caution is repeated. What kind of person, I wondered, would risk letting their dog pee on the Queen's curtains? ('I'm very sorry your Majesty but we'll get you some new ones . . .')

The room is full of ornate silver sculptures, housed in glass cases, and lined with paintings. Hanging here is *The Connoisseurs*, a self-portrait of the celebrated landscape artist Sir Edwin Landseer who is pictured flanked by two earnest-looking dogs. They peer over both his shoulders from a dark background, more like parents than pets. Landseer is sitting; the dogs might be on their hind legs. Another painting shows a chow standing imperiously among some condiments: *Marco on the Queen's Breakfast Table* by C.B. Barber.

'They can be very pesky dogs,' said an American woman looking up at the painting.

Marco belonged to Queen Victoria, a dog-lover like Elizabeth II. Beyond the castle is a dedicated dog-walking trail where you find another statue marked: *NOBLE. FOR MORE THAN 15 YEARS THE FAVOURITE COLLIE AND DEAR COMPANION OF QUEEN VICTORIA.*

The road west of the castle is surfaced and ideal for putting along. Far from the throng of tourists, I ran into Anne and Frank McDermott from Buckinghamshire. Frank looked like a golfer – tall, tanned, polo shirt, chinos, relaxed gait, ready smile – and sure enough they had come to Scotland to watch the Open and play a little.

'Things have changed,' said Frank of the championship. 'When I watched Nick Faldo at Muirfield a dozen of us were able to follow him round at six in the morning. Now, what with Tiger . . . I think they're going to have to make it 'ticket only', like the Masters.'

Frank, whose grandfather was a farmer, also expressed concern over the plans to ban hunting with dogs.

'Have you ever heard a fox cub crying?' he asked. 'They sound just like a baby.' He found this eerie, and not endearing. 'My grandfather had a fox in his chicken coup. It killed the lot, about 80 of them. Didn't eat any.'

I'd heard this said before but always thought it was part of the demonisation; a pretext for persecution. Prejudice is often passed down between families, sometimes in the guise of folklore. If Frank's granddad wasn't exaggerating, then the wanton killing he described makes the fox even more like the shooters. (Estates, after all, make their money primarily from the destruction of the grouse, not from the sale of its strong, stringy meat.)

A mile or so further on I let rip a sumptuous five-wood, flying it to the left of the road where I found it sitting up in some grass, 180 yards away. The tarmac gave way to stones and sand but it was still possible to putt with the tennis ball. A footpath used as a shortcut was bumpier but the pines bordering it were short, and again I could play an iron. I'd enjoyed a few of these breaks. On the hill, for example, the wind strengthens as you climb higher but the heather invariably recedes, allowing you to switch from football back to golf ball.

A red squirrel hopped across the path and a spiralled up a tree, moving with the staccato agility of a lizard.

The pretty animals of the forest wouldn't see a Top Flite fizzing through the branches. A shanked ball could obliterate a squirrel which is a protected species. However, the odds of that happening must have ranked alongside my winning the Open. There's a certain conceit about imagining yourself beset by freakish accidents; in thinking you are destined to be the one-in-a-million who dies in a plane crash, for example. All neurotics are vainglorious; they fret about being ordinary. They have a morbid fear of living; of being amassed. I was no more likely to knock a squirrel from the trees than find myself in court for leaving trail of broken farming machinery across the North-east. I flung another eight-iron along the track.

The sun had burned through the morning cloud, fraying it at the edges like a fag against cloth. Flies, some as fat as raisins, followed like a royal entourage. The golf bag chafed my left shoulder beneath a thin T-shirt. My left palm was badly blistered at the base of the ring finger. I was wearing tracksuit bottoms with zipping pockets and a water-repellent finish – great for stumbling through wet heather but hardly summer wear. The heavy, black cloth soaked up the heat. I just had to take them off.

So there I was, walking through the Balmoral Estate in my underpants and matching checked cap, playing golf. All my tetchiness had gone, the blue-brown River Dee was below and the snowy corries of Beinn A'Bhuird were ahead. I joined the A93 just beyond Invercauld Bridge after 384 shots. Prince Andrew had missed a beautiful day's golf . . .

| STROKES: 384 | TOTAL: 3850 | SCORE: -495 |
| --- | --- | --- |

# The Open

*20 July 2000.* Tiger Woods. Second shot to the sixth. Sand wedge. The ball follows a singularly peculiar trajectory, more like a drive. Even the strike sounds different to those players around him. 'It'll bite,' says a spectator. It runs through the back of the green, perilously close to some gorse. Tiger – slighter than they might have anticipated, small boyish face – has fluffed his shot, thinned it. He is transparently human, which just makes the rest of his play all the more remarkable. That drive, for example – with a 'chopped-down' three-wood according to his caddie. During practice he also put the ball through the back of the green. Off the tee. On this 412-yard hole.

## ELEVEN

# Better than any TV Programme

| HOLE 11 | DISTANCE: 7 MILES | PAR: 438 |
| --- | --- | --- |

THE MOST engaging part of Paul Lawrie's 1999 Open win didn't take place on the Carnoustie course. It was what happened next. Paul drives himself home, Claret Jug in the back seat of his Saab, cradled in a cardboard box. Arriving in Aberdeen, he sits down to watch a video of himself winning the Open. And then, when he and his wife find they can't sleep, she does some ironing and he *potters around the garage* . . .

I'd hoped to pick up some tips from Paul when I passed Meldrum House Golf Club on my way through Oldmeldrum. He is the club's touring professional and practises there on his own range. That he didn't reply to my letter wasn't altogether surprising. Ten minutes of Paul's time is rather less than ten minutes of my own when shared among the hundreds clamouring for a piece of it.

Polite letters were also sent to Oldmeldrum, Alford and Braemar golf clubs. I explained what I was up to and asked if the secretary or professional or some other luminary would care to join me for a round and a blether about the game's seductive charm. Balmoral alone had the courtesy to say bugger off. Perhaps some cumbersome committees have yet to formulate and ratify a reply.

Contrast this with the United States. A few years back I was on the Pebble Beach peninsula in California, hung-over, scruffy and searching for breakfast. I stopped at Spyglass Hill, a course which is ranked 34th in that huge country and is among the top 60 in the world. The professional there, Mark Brenneman, heard my accent, reminisced about playing in Scotland and told me to grab a buggy and check out the course of which he was justifiably proud. At a club of similar prestige in Britain I'd have probably been shown the door.

Ian Stewart-Grant had told me that he was reported to his club's committee for *laughing* on the course. That clubs have been slow to get involved with the Scottish Executive's golf initiative was foreseeable. Some exist for their own glorification, not the greater good. They are chauvinist, cliquish and bogged down in the minutiae of the game. Maybe that's why I've never had the urge to join a club and instead spend my time on municipal courses: because I want to play golf.

The Isle of Skye Golf Club at Sconser is my kind of club. Members of the public are welcome to play. It has a nine-hole course and an eighteen-hole course, an impressive feat of architecture when there are only nine greens. Those on the '18-hole' use a second set of tees and have right of way.

Golf on Skye is more laid-back than on the mainland. The greenkeeper, for example, continued to mow grass within a few yards of where I was putting. Who was I to demand silence? I watched the imperturbable Tiger Woods tee off during this year's Open as jets from RAF Leuchars rent the air above. Those who look for distraction look for excuses.

I've never putted better than I did that day at Skye. I hadn't gone to the island to play golf and was using hired clubs. The putter – a Regal Goose – didn't belong to the set and I asked the club steward if he would trade this old, rather worn club for a new one. Fraser MacKinnon readily agreed. Nowhere on the island sold clubs so I bought one in Aberdeen and sent it in. Within a week the putter arrived with a kind letter thanking me for 'a very fair exchange'. I carry the 'wee gold one', as Fraser called it, in my bag as a second putter but rarely use it, and never on consecutive holes. As a charm, it provides confidence. As a tool, it might end up sullying the memory of that day on Skye . . .

After a short walk along the A93 (which I treated as a drop) I picked up a path that crosses the southern flank of Creag Choinnich into Braemar. It weaves through a dank pine wood which is quilted with mosses and lichens. A sign asks you to keep to the path. Invercauld Estate and North East Native Woodlands drafted a plan for regenerating native pine and birch on the neighbouring hill. This involved killing the rabbits and deer that feed voraciously on the seedlings; a cull paid for by the Forestry Commission. Fencing here is a poor solution because capercaillie and other wildlife can become entangled in it.

The route slices across a steep slope – down which my tennis ball kept rolling – carrying me above a birch-filled gorge. Invercauld House sits across the river from here.

The heather had started to flower behind it, casting a regal purple cloak across the shoulders of the hills. In late summer, when the sun-soaked hills reach ignition point, this Brillo-pad of a plant bursts forth with lambent splendour. Cygnet-into-swan doesn't compare.

The path became like a putting green. I punched a couple of decadent nine-irons high above the trees before the wood again closed in. One hundred and twenty-six shots brought me into Braemar.

Every September around 18,000 people cram the village here for the Braemar Gathering. The tradition stretches back more than 1,000 years when Highland Games were held under the sponsorship of kings and clan chiefs, and combined a variety of martial, sporting and religious functions. It was a chance for Clansmen to show off. At the Braemar Gathering the Queen takes the salute, fulfilling a role assumed by an ancient ancestor of hers in the eleventh century. Back then, King Malcolm arranged a hill-race the winner of which was recruited to his ranks as a footrunner.

Some Highland Games now attract commercial sponsorship but the individual prize money is rarely more than a few hundred pounds and there are only a handful of full-time professionals in Scotland.

# PAR 10,000

To boost participation, Highland Council tried introducing caber-tossing to the primary school sports curriculum a few years ago. Twenty-one feet of larch was replaced with six feet of foam rubber. The Scottish Association of Highland Games was lukewarm about the recruitment drive, describing it as 'fallacy' to use a foam rubber caber. Technique, it said, was more important than brute strength – though it did admit it might be foolhardy to hand a telegraph pole to a child.

The present day gathering features athletics, dancing and piping. Around a dozen bands take part. Many people are there to watch the Queen and this has rejuvenated the games just as the spectacle of Billy Connolly in a kilt has rejuvenated those held at Lonach, held a few miles from Connolly's home to the north of Deeside. His friend Robin Williams also packs a running vest and turns up. Even as a youngster the Queen never took part, but her enthusiasm is genuine.

'The feedback we get seems to suggest the Royals enjoy it,' explained William Meston, secretary of the Braemar Royal Highland Society for 22 years. 'You can tell from their expressions. We get a letter of thanks from Balmoral every year, and one from the Queen Mother.'

And what do you suppose is her favourite event? The caber-tossing? The hill race, packed as it is with historical import?

'The kids' sack race. She just loves that.'

I had decided to putt along the road that runs six miles from Braemar to the Linn of Dee. While the river basin below is very flat, the Dee's course is drunken. It lurches one way then the other, each kink and curve shored up by a bank of white pebbles. Flooding here is welcomed. Work is going on to reconstitute the alluvial wetlands beloved by many birds. It may have looked like a fairway from above, but I'd have ended up with wet feet and no balls within a mile.

As a young hillwalker I detested this road. It stands before the Cairngorms like a bouncer, checking out the fitness of those making for the hills on foot. On the way back I resented it even more. I'd shuffle along in silence, yards apart from my equally knackered companions, thumb hung out behind in the hope of hitching a lift, the party over. The Post Bus, if it was about, was a god-send. Today you can still ride with the mail.

After a few miles I passed *Roaring Stag*, a roadside house. During my brief stint as a ghillie I stayed here when the Mar estate owned it. Now it is home to Pam and Peter Thackrah.

'We're so grateful to be living here,' said Pam. 'There's so much birdlife. It's better than any TV programme. We embrace it every day.'

# BETTER THAN ANY TV PROGRAMME

The Thackrahs moved north from Greater Manchester. They became smitten with the area many years ago after visiting Mar Lodge. In those days it had a bar that served venison burgers, much to the surprise and delight of the Thackrah's two sons. The house lies at 1,250 feet; there's an elevation mark on the western wall. The couple are about to undertake a regeneration project of their own by creating a garden from native plants. 'It won't be easy with the rabbits,' said Pam.

Their neighbour is Willie Forbes, a former keeper on the Mar Lodge estate and a stalker of near mythic status. I used to hear tales about Willie when I worked on the Mar estate – how he had pursued a wounded stag long into the night, his feral instinct allowing him to draw close enough to dispatch it. He is also a very fine painter and taxidermist, an alchemist who in two dimensions can capture the dynamism of a grouse in flight, and in three can resurrect the dead. Willie must know his wildlife inside out.

'He's Scotland's best kept secret,' said Pam. Unfortunately Willie wasn't home.

'He's away playing golf,' added Peter.

I caught up with Willie Forbes later on the phone. He had indeed been playing golf and bemoaned his handicap of 18.

'Rubbish . . .' he said. 'I've been that for a long time and never improved. If you want to get down to ten you'd have to give up work and play golf all the time.'

Willie talks with a genial growl. His manner is bluff, irreverent. As a stalker he was happy to uplift weary hillwalkers in his Land-rover, saving them the trudge back to their car, but only if they had stayed clear of the deer during the day.

'If not, I'd leave them to walk,' he said. 'Wouldn't have mattered if they had blisters, or half their leg missing . . . Most folk were understanding, though. There was plenty of room for the stalkers and hillwalkers to work around each other. There was no need for anybody to start shouting about being in the way.'

His real work starts at the end of autumn when dozens of stag heads arrive to be mounted. He has also recently started making moulds for bronze statues. 'I'm kept busy but I still get about,' he said. 'I do a bit of pig-shooting in Germany.'

As for the changes on the hill he says: 'More fences, more people, heavier culls, no grouse. But it's always been changing, from the start. The rifles have changed from when I started stalking. You've got these rocket launchers now . . . It's maybe too late for pine forests to come back. The soil's stricken. I've seen trees that look like bonsai.'

This is said without regret or reproach. I suspect that in his art, Scotland's best-kept secret, reflects exactly what he sees, in all its seething glory and horror and amorality.

Not everyone is enamoured with village life. Those who grow up in a place like Braemar discover jobs are few and far between and the cost of travel – and increasingly property – is beyond them. Many houses are bought as holiday or retirement homes. The new owners often pay well over the odds, certainly more than many a young local family can afford.

Local authorities continue to unload council-housing stock and cottages get snapped up quickly. Prof. Mark Shucksmith of Aberdeen University has described a 'lack of social housing' as 'the most important issue facing rural communities'. Even if the political will existed to build again, finding space could be difficult. Land reforms are expected to address this.

Shucksmith, who works with Arkleton Centre for Rural Development Research, estimates that up to one in three rural dwellers may experience poverty. Don't let the lack of slums here fool you. Restricted public transport, dependency on the car, high fuel prices, low pay, low pensions, a lack of unionisation – all these things conspire to make life a trial. Rural dwellers are also poorly informed about social benefits and less inclined to claim them because of the attendant stigma.

That's the trouble with a tight-knit community. It fans pernicious gossip and heightens the sense of isolation among those who stand outside it.

The elderly are especially susceptible to poverty. Those who retire to the countryside may be remote from their immediate family, leaving them without routine support should they become frail. The elderly already in the area are in the same vulnerable position if their family has moved away in search of jobs and affordable housing.

The Government has recognised rural deprivation as being distinct from that in urban areas where job opportunities, housing choices and support networks such as training and childcare facilities are broader. In a joint report to the Scottish Executive this summer, Shucksmith claimed:

> The powerful myth of a rural idyll, in which 'rural' and 'exclusion' are often seen as a contradiction in terms, combined with the lack of solidarity and the greater visibility of exclusion

in small communities, often means that the poor people in rural areas unwittingly conspire with the more affluent to hide their poverty and deny its existence . . . Community development initiatives have tended to neglect the distinction between 'communities of interest' and 'communities of place' which is so important in rural areas. Consequently, area-based attempts at community development in rural areas have tended to reinforce rather than relieve social exclusion by redistributing power to the already powerful who tend to dominate local initiatives.

Of course you could argue that this is the trade-off for clean air and not having to padlock your bike outside shops. Even if they could afford to stay, many youngsters wouldn't. Village life can be stultifying, embarrassing even. The things that attract retired couples to a place like Braemar – pubs without music, other old folk – drive the young away.

You tend not to appreciate what's on your own doorstep, even when it's something as conspicuously amazing as the Cairngorms. After visiting the Pyrenees I was struck less by the rocky grandeur of the range than by the realisation of what a great place I'd left behind. In Tobago I met a Liverpool couple who urged me to visit the Argyll falls that tumble through the world's oldest protected rainforest. Frankly, I've seen more impressive cataracts ten miles from Aberdeen. They had travelled 5,000 miles to reach Tobago but had never explored Scotland.

Sadly, that's also true of many Scots. I was gobsmacked when I first drove through Ross-shire and Sutherland. The journey doesn't begin properly until you reach Inverness. Kessock Bridge hangs in the mid-distance, slung between the Highland capital and the Black Isle like a rope bridge leading to an older, more dramatic world – where the land bubbles, throwing up shards of ever more improbable mountain. If you've never been, go in early spring or late autumn when the hills have a splash of snow and the midges are either side of life.

The Linn of Dee road was a fine place for golf. You can fairly crack a tennis ball with a putter. If you swing it like an iron it's possible to lift the ball through the air. One of my shots landed in some thistles and another over a deer fence, but otherwise the ball went more or less straight. The fat, black flies had returned (I recognised their faces), spreading out behind my head like a vortex as I jogged between shots. The harder I ran, the harder they chased. It was probably the sweat drawing them on.

# PAR 10,000

The 228th shot carried me over the Dee towards Mar Lodge. I stopped on the bridge and gazed down into the pellucid, peat-stained water, expecting to see some fish.

Every year salmon return to spawn in the river from the far coast of Greenland. They must outwit birds, otters, seals and sharks. They must avoid the capacious nets of Greenland's fishermen, yet more nets in the North and Irish seas and at the mouths of rivers – as well as the angler and his rod. And then there are the poachers who wait on the banks with their poisons and nets and cages and refrigerated lorries.

Many Scottish rivers report half the catches of 40 years ago. Back then, the Dee 'ran silver' in spring. Today, only one out of every 2,500 hatchlings makes it back to its birthplace. Mechanised fishing is largely responsible but angling too has been detrimental, picking off the vital survivors. Many riparian owners on the Dee have been forced to operate a catch-and-release policy. Only the first fish caught can be kept – but then how can anyone be sure that the one 'for the pot' isn't the last one in the river?

What I remember most about growing up on the Dee was the birdlife, those truly expert fishers. A heron, hunched motionless at the river's edge; a cormorant standing tall, its wings held out to dry; a tern moving above the surface as though on strings; a merganser on the water, head submerged, watching for trout and par, later reappearing many yards from where it dived. And once a kingfisher, a blue light flashing across the burn where I had cast a worm. The water bailiff discovered the young in a sandbank. 'Ugly brown little fellows', he called them.

Sometimes the fish got their own back on the birds. Over a summer week I watched a clutch of moorhen chicks disappear one by one – some taken by mink but others by pike – until finally the mother bird was alone and her loud, resonant 'kirrick' went unanswered among the reeds of that deadly backwater.

The problem with Mar Lodge is that it keeps bursting into flames. Every hundred years or so it goes up like a volcano. The first conflagration happened in 1895. You're always warned not to return to a burning building for *any* possession. The Duke of Fife somehow managed to retrieve 3,000 sets of antlers. Or rather his gallant staff did. (Still, you can't help feeling it might have been braver to disobey his orders.) His wife, Queen Victoria's granddaughter, sketched the new lodge, which lasted until 1991 when it too went up in smoke. It belonged to media tycoon John Kluge, then one of America's richest men, and was being renovated at the time. (Kluge bought Mar Lodge as a wedding present for his third wife, Patricia, who was keen to have the Queen for a neighbour.)

The new owners, the National Trust for Scotland, will let you an apartment for around £200 a week. Mar Lodge is pretty enough with its red pan-tiles and latticed windows and wide-flung wings, but it could pass for a nursing home. I avoided its mock-Tudor embrace and jogged along the road.

The air had curdled in the sultry afternoon heat and was best taken in gulps. Dense, black clouds had gathered above the southern Grampians, their tendrils hanging like dreadlocks. I've often willed a churning summer storm to throw down a tornado. (Not an F5 obviously, just something to knock your hat off.) A twister has the same compelling horror as a road smash. It is Mother Nature's umbilical, whipping around between heaven and earth, the meteorological equivalent of a shark's fin on the horizon.

Rain splatted the tarmac. The sky started to flicker and crackle. And there I was, beneath some trees, waving a metal rod in the air. Small wonder golfers account for a *fifth* of people killed by lightning in the United States. In his book *Mountain Leadership*, Eric Langmuir writes:

> Lightning strikes tend to be concentrated on mountain tops and other natural projections. Since points 'service' a fairly wide area, there tends to be a shaded or relatively safe zone associated with them. The peak must be at least seven metres high and the relative safety zone is of the same order horizontally.

(A more accurate guide to how lightning might behave is provided by calculating the attenuation and phase velocity as a function of frequency for the ambient electron and ion densities, using appropriate values for ground conductivity and permitivity and the ambient magnetic field, but as I didn't have a calculator handy I just played on.)

After 328 strokes I reached the start of the Lairig Ghru. Six hundred and five under par is the kind of advantage you need be to carrying into Britain's biggest mountain range . . .

**STROKES: 328       TOTAL: 4178       SCORE: -605**

# Birdies and Bogeys

If, on a hole, you take one stroke less than the par, this is known as a 'birdie'. Two under is called an 'eagle' and three under an 'albatross'. The terms, coined in the United States, are thought to reflect how well the ball carries through the air – an albatross has an even bigger wingspan than an eagle. A 'pterodactyl' might represent a hole-in-one at a par five, but as nobody has pulled this off the name is not yet in common usage. A 'bogey' is a British name for a score one over par. The origin of this is uncertain. It may to relate to trains, as in: 'that ball was moving like it had a truck of ore attached to it'. Two over par is known unimaginatively as a 'double-bogey'. A 'sleeper' (as in a long-haul locomotive) might find more favour among poor players keen to enjoy the colourful terminology associated with scoring. One day you might hear a golfer remarking: 'I had a bogey at the sixth, a sleeper at the seventh and a derailment [triple bogey] at the eighth.'

# TWELVE

# The Long Walk In

I LEFT the car in a lay-by where the Lairig Ghru – the main route through the Cairngorms – spits you out after 18 miles. A woman in charge of a nearby campsite said the police would 'keep an eye' on it and gave me a form to fill out. It asked for details about the vehicle, my route and any equipment carried.

Head Torch? No.

Emergency food? No.

Whistle? No.

Waterproof Clothing? No.

Polybag? No.

When you're golfing across mountains you need to get your priorities right. A ready supply of balls is more important than a pack-lunch or an ice-axe.

I'd found a driving range that sold batches of 300 old balls for £25. The dimples were worn smooth and some had chunks missing, but they still flew better than my football. I'd also invested in a military-style waistcoat with 14 pockets and space for over 100 balls. Loaded up, it felt like a flak jacket. Before setting off I put five bananas, a cheese sandwich and two litres of water in my stomach (a handy place for storing food and drink, I find). The football hung from my shorts in a plastic bag, swaying like a beaver's tail.

Choosing a club was difficult. A wood is best for heather, a putter for tracks. On balance I reckoned a seven-iron would get the most out of the Top Flite XL Super Range balls, which would carry at least 100 yards.

Five years ago the National Trust for Scotland paid many millions for Mar Lodge and the 75,000 acres of garden that include the Cairngorms.

# PAR 10,000

Understandably, the charity is very protective of the mountain range. A pine trunk blocks vehicular access to Derry Lodge. Signs tell you not to mountain bike, not to light fires, not to leave litter and not to get shot.

Fortunately they say nothing about golf.

That's probably because no one has ever attempted to swing a club in the Cairngorms, and with good reason. The wind here once gusted to 172 mph. That wouldn't just play havoc with your driving but could punt you and your bag across the sky too. (*And Tiger Woods has ended up in a tree. But where has his ball gone . . . ?*) The plateau has more in common with the arctic than the Old Course, yet to look at them you would never guess the Cairngorms is the biggest mountain range in Britain. Even under snow some of these bulky hills look no more prepossessing than a half-eaten meringue. They aren't the sort of mountains you might prick yourself on. No – they kill by stealth.

If you're lost on a ridge a few yards wide (a typical west-coast scenerio) there are only two directions in which you can die, and both are perpendicular to the ridge. Blindfolded, there's a 50–50 chance you'll grope your way to safety. In the Cairngorms every bearing can take you into trouble because losing height is so difficult. The plateau, much of it above 1,000 metres, could comfortably accommodate a small town, complete with a multiplex and a B&Q. Gentle contours can hold you in the same suffocating embrace as a spider's web. You can quickly find yourself immobilised by mist, paralysed by snow, hypnotised by spindrift, thoroughly alienated from your own senses – before the wind rushes in to finish you off. These mountains may resemble a whipped egg, but they also have fangs.

The track to Derry Lodge is hard-packed. I cringed whenever I struck a ball, expecting the club-head to snap, and tended to keep to half-swings. Beyond the Lui Water, a rippling meadow opens out to the left of the path – a links course with soft, dry peat hags for bunkers. My ball landed with a thump and was relatively easy to find among the short grass, heather and tree stumps. I reached Derry Lodge – boarded up, very 'Hammer horror' – after 110 shots.

Three tents were pitched there – one with mountain bikes lying outside in flagrant defiance of the National Trust's commitment to preserving 'the spirit of the long walk in'.

The National Trust was established by an Act of Parliament nearly 70 years ago to guard the nation's heritage of architectural, scenic and historic treasures. Today it cares for more than 100 buildings and nearly 200,000 acres of countryside, and is the fourth biggest landowner in

Scotland. (The Forestry Commission is comfortably the biggest with one and a half million acres.) A few members of the British aristocracy still survive in this top ten but those lower down have been displaced by foreigners who pay handsomely for drafty castles and unprofitable areas of heather.

When the Trust took charge of the Mar estate in 1995 it promised the 'conservation of the natural heritage qualities of Mar Lodge estate' would 'take priority over field sports'. However, charging people to shoot stags helps cover the estimated £300,000 annual running costs.

The National Trust's mission throughout Scotland is to 'keep things just as they are', which means doing plenty. Ponds, for example, need dredging to stop them silting up with dead vegetation and turning into marsh (not a problem if new ones were allowed to form elsewhere). The Trust also aims to restore 'lost or damaged communities of plants and landscape features'.

Seven thousand years ago the Mar area was covered with Scots pine. By the mid-seventeenth century the whole of Donside and the fertile lower parts of the Dee and Spey had been turned into fields. Just over 100 years later, timber from hillsides was being floated down the rivers and turned into ships. Cheap timber imports discouraged the replanting of trees. Woodland now covers only 12 per cent of the Cairngorms.

According to the Forestry Commission, deer densities over much of the range are 'well in excess' of those which would allow natural regeneration of trees. In the last 30 years the population has increased by a third and group sizes are among the highest in the world. The Cairngorms has over 40,000 red deer, one fifth of Scotland's population. The Commission suggests that, 'deer numbers could be markedly reduced whilst still allowing estates to take a similar cull' – and that 'better forage availability [in woodland] would enhance the condition of the remaining deer'. However, it concludes:

> These benefits would be partly offset by a greater difficulty in stalking within woodland areas as compared to the open hill. Furthermore, any major change from open-hill stalking to woodland-based stalking may remove one of the key reasons why many paying clients currently come to shoot deer in Scotland rather than other parts of Europe.

You might question why Mar is being run as a sporting estate at all. Such estates are understandably reluctant to cull too many deer. It's like asking a shop-owner to discard some of his stock. Some sporting estates feed deer through the winter rather than allowing the cold to pick off the old and infirm. The Trust has put up fences to protect trees here, but this is a poor compromise that endangers birds like the capercaillie and black grouse which can become entangled in it. You don't see any such fences on the RSBP's Abernethy estate – but then you don't see nearly as many deer either.

At Derry Lodge I found five young walkers from Arbroath heaving rucksacks onto their backs. They were heading for Loch 'Lui'. I think they meant Loch A'an but were too busy flicking persistent midges from their faces to talk further. In a one-to-one situation the walker has little to fear from these tiny blood-sucking gnats. The trouble is, they rarely hang out in groups of less than 10,000.

All sorts of protection has been devised – a bracelet impregnated with lemon juice, spectacles which pump air out of the frames, a 'mechanical lung' which exhales carbon dioxide and lures the midges into a vacuum trap. Few work. Creams, for example, can leave you repellent only to friends. A bee-keeping hat made from muslin can afford some protection, but unfortunately it also makes you look like a prat.

More encouragingly, researchers at Aberdeen University have discovered that the midge has an 'aggregation pheromone' – a scent that flags up the feast to other midges. They are hoping to identify the pheromone and use this in a trap. They are also trying to figure out why a midge should turn up its proboscis at people like me (something to do with the body masking attractive chemicals) and make straight for others instead.

Beyond Derry Lodge the Lairig becomes rockier. Where it crosses the Luibeg water, young pines grow like cacti among friable boulders and gravel. The trees and the burn are surrounded by a deer fence, which makes the whole scene look like a garden centre.

Although the trees weren't staked, I allowed myself a 'free drop' on the far side of the fence where the Lairig climbs steeply over the southern slope of Carn a' Mhaim. Because the path is full of crests and dips, some of which might have contained walkers, I switched to the tennis ball. Within quarter of a mile I had caught up with two walkers who kept stopping to consult a map. The chance to play through came when they sat down on a boulder.

Meeting other walkers on a hill can be awkward. On summits you stand around like strangers at party, waiting to touch the cairn, and then

### THE FIRST TEE
One of Scotland's biggest bunkers – otherwise known as Balmedie Beach on the east coast. © Anna Henly

### WATER HAZARD
'Casual water' was much easier to avoid than some of the obstacles found in fields. © Anna Henly

### READY TO RUN

Checking escape routes in the fields above Balmoral Castle.
© Anna Henly

### CULTURE CLASH

A monument to the Battle of Harlaw, one of the bloodiest battles between Highlanders and Lowlanders. © Anna Henly

**ENGAGING**
The much-loved public toilets in Pitmedden after their closure by the local authority.
© Anna Henly

**ROAD RUNNER**
Heading through Strathdon on the rebound from Scar Hill.
© Anna Henly

**SINKING FEELING**

Mulling over the threat to farm machinery
from golf balls in the Vale Hotel, Alford.
© Anna Henly

**BED FOR THE NIGHT**

Approaching what might yet be the
18th green at Pittodrie House hotel.
© Anna Henly

## A HIGHLAND WELCOME

John and Isobel MacBean extended their hospitality to a hungry golfer.

## ROUGH TALK

Robert Rothney describes the peculiar difficulties
of playing through 'set-aside' land.
© Anna Henly

**TIGER WATCH OUT**
One of Scotland's poorest golfers in action.
© Anna Henly

**CALLING A CAB**
Taxis were suprisingly easy to come by in the smallest villages. © Anna Henly

**NEVER SAFE**
A bale of hay is one of the many dangers lurking in the countryside . . .
© Anna Henly

## IN THE ROUGH
The woods around Bennachie are more testing for the golfer than the hill itself.
© Anna Henly

## A BLESSING
The Rev. Canon David Day, who would encourage us to see God in a wider way.

slink away. Some are full of bonhomie, gushing 'hellos', comparing notes, sharing the occasional sandwich. I find this kind of camaraderie somewhat forced, given the huge numbers of people up here in search of solitude, some of them resentful of one another's presence.

The couple watched silently as I addressed the tennis ball. Whenever someone lets you overtake them on a golf course, you always hope to hit a decent shot as they dutifully wait their turn. You will have probably already harried them, sent the ball snapping at their heels, stood with your hands on your hips to convey your impatience and superiority. You don't want to end up in the bushes. Unfortunately I topped the tennis ball. It struck a boulder and took off high above my head. I had to ask the couple where it landed.

Typically, the shots that *followed* were all good ones. I had learned another trick: wet a tennis ball and it flies straighter. The path from here became bumpier still. There were patches of gravel and peat to play from, but sometimes I had to carry the ball among the giant cobbles before I could find a lie. Four hundred shots brought me fully into the Lairig Ghru.

As I rounded Carn a' Mhaim a fine perfume of rain blew towards me. A rainbow arched across the triangular cliff-face of the Devil's Point; the perfect logo for this new fragrance: '*Lairig* – with a hint of heather'.

So far, so good.

---

**STROKES: 400     TOTAL: 4578     SCORE: -643**

---

## *'Fore!'*

Golf courses throughout the country resound to the cry of 'Fore!'. A player shouts this warning when his ball is heading in the direction of others. If the ball looks likely to miss them by several feet it's probably best to shout nothing. Otherwise, they will adopt a semi-crouch and scuttle forwards or backwards straight into the path of the ball. (Note: this won't keep them from being indignant over your silence.) On hearing 'Fore!' you should adopt the brace position recommended by airlines – that is: drop to the ground with your hands and arms clasped around your head. This, however, is a rare sight on courses, as most golfers would rather preserve the creases in their trousers than the bone around their brain. They will merely flap their hands around their heads, as though trying to buffer themselves against sudden downpour, not a projectile that has more in common with a bullet.

## THIRTEEN

# A Protection Racket

| HOLE 13 | DISTANCE: 15 MILES | PAR: 937 |
|---------|--------------------|----------|

FOUR OUT OF Scotland's five highest mountains rise either side of the Lairig Ghru. It is quite open in its lower reaches but you still have to crane your head back to behold all 4,235 feet of Cairn Toul rising like a volcano, its deep-bowled corries often swimming with cloud.

In contrast, Corrour Bothy on the Lairig floor shapes up like a potting shed. Still, Corrour must be one of Britain's toughest buildings. I've stayed here when the temperature dipped to -23 °C. Water collected from the nearby burn developed a skin of ice before I returned to the bothy. I could have melted some snow – there was plenty lying around inside – but the freezing conditions sapped the pressure from my gas stove. It could barely raise a flame.

I was now level with the bothy. The Lairig continued to move like a wave along the side of Ben Macdui. In the troughs I could switch to proper golf balls. Sometimes the ball would bounce back onto the path or come to rest among the grass and bluebells at its side. I had met only three people coming the other way – an English holiday-maker with his young son and a lone walker with a towering rucksack and a mini-disk player strapped to his wrist. Perhaps he was listening to something soothing, like whale songs.

Up here, 80 miles from its mouth, the River Dee is just another burn. With every step it grows smaller and noisier and more fickle – a sort of regression. The Lairig rises here towards a tumult of pink boulders over which a tributary rushes. I was forced to deploy the football, hugging the heather above the path until the slope became too rocky to play on.

I had reached the Pools of Dee: dregs from the Ice Age. These diminutive turquoise lochans seem too geometrical for this shadowy, unmade place, looking more like the features you might find in a shopping centre. You can almost picture a fountain and some coins on the bottom of the three pools, maybe some goldfish. The water is clear, preternaturally so, but then you can't see the atmospheric pollutants that fall upon our mountains like bleach. It was less easy to miss the discarded Mars Bars wrappers and beer bottles lying on the banks. Who walks all this way to drop litter? They diminish their own wilderness experience as well as that of others.

So too, it must be said, does golf. Scotland's biggest mountain range was reduced for me to a 'lateral hazard'. I had found myself thinking less about the glacier that ploughed this colossal furrow than about the need to keep my left arm straight and my wrists cocked. The kind of clothes that facilitate a clean swing (that is, as few as possible) also appear contemptuous of the mountains and their weather.

But if I was under-dressed for the Cairngorms, then many walkers here are over-dressed. In August you don't need heavy boots or an arctic fleece or a rucksack packed with chocolate and naval flares. Such accoutrements are mere props, but then some people don't want to hear that. When you pay two hundred pounds for a kagoule, you are buying into a rugged outdoor illusion.

Golf is every bit as fetishistic as hillwalking. To be honest, I'd have been very glad of a kagoule at the 2,733 foot top of the pass and I regretted not carrying one. It wouldn't have weighed more than a few golf balls. The wind rattled around the corries and left me shivering as I started the long descent towards Rothiemurchus. On days like this the Lairig is no place to linger. The scale of it alone can depress you. Screes run red off the hillside at the top of the cleft; Lurcher's Crag and other cliffs close above you like bloodied jaws. God, it was miserable.

The Cairngorms are the coldest, windiest place in Britain and gather more snow than any other mountain range. During the festive season skiers arrive like a flock of migrant birds to fan out across the slopes, their jinking movements reminiscent of a mating dance. The modern skier has grown bored making repetitive runs down the same stretch of mountain and people are venturing off-piste in search of the type of thrills enjoyed 30 years earlier. In those days the snow's cover lasted from October to April. You didn't have to make your own as people do now.

On the summit of Cairn Gorm there's a restaurant, The Ptarmigan, named after the bird displaced to build it. You gain the top by straddling some granite paving stones that are as crass as plastic flowers. Paths and tows scarify the mountain. The soil has been compacted by skiers, leading to flooding further down the hillside. Erosion blights the lower slopes, creating weeping sores. Cairn Gorm is like a mob killing: kicked senseless, lacerated, tied up with wire, doused with acid rain. A vendetta may have been launched here. The 90 foot crane being used to construct a funicular railway was temporarily sidelined after somehow becoming damaged . . . I'm quite surprised eco-warriors haven't vandalised the ski-centre before now. They could perhaps tear up the rubber foot mats and replace them with irregular boulders. A few pot plants placed outside the restaurant might soften its austere concrete entrance.

Developers here do their bit, though, to appease the vociferous environmental lobby. As I write, the fifteen million pound Cairn Gorm Mountain Railway (due for completion in 2002) won't allow passengers to disembark at the top and go wandering off across the plateau. Hillwalkers, I suspect, are delighted. They would rather have the Cairngorms all to themselves. The corries, the cliffs, the rare Alpine plants . . . If anybody is going to trample *silene acaulis*, let it be someone who knows its scientific name for God's sake. That's the feeling you get, anyway.

You could argue mountains are there to be used up. Scientists give the sun just five billion years, within which time God is sure to hook an asteroid our way.

It was quarter of a mile before I could again hit the football – a 50-stroke penalty. A slice dropped the ball down into a burn, out of sight of the path. As I clambered down to fetch it, I found myself clinging to the heather like a child on a teat. It was a relief to regain the path. When you walk alone you are especially careful how you tread. Going solo sharpens your movement and your mind. You can't cheat yourself about your abilities. It's that same self-reliance that makes golf such an absorbing game.

If I'd slipped and broken an ankle and lain by the burn for days, I doubt the mountain rescue team would have been chuffed. Stern public warnings would have been issued: the Cairngorms are no place for golf. If I had died I might have become the star of an apocryphal tale, one successive generations could have embellished with addition of a faithful caddie, found holding an umbrella above us both when we perished, mid-swing, in that freak autumnal blizzard at the turn of the millennium.

Rescue teams, led by police, receive no Government support. Members must buy their own gear – waterproofs, ice-axes, ropes. The RAF provides helicopter cover but the downsizing of military bases means it's only a matter of time before Scotland's 26 rescue teams are required to bring along their own Sea Kings. On the Continent professional teams retrieve the dead and injured. They instinctively check a casualty's pockets first, not his pulse, for vital signs of insurance. (Back in Britain, teams are strongly opposed to this 'professionalisation', despite being called upon to save walkers so incompetent they should be wearing a red ball on their nose.)

So why *volunteer* for mountain rescue work? Altruism? Because the brush with death piques your sense of being alive? Or because you get to ride in a helicopter, handle walkie-talkies and behave like Robert Duval in *Apocalypse Now*? Given that vanity is behind most things in life, probably the latter.

I'm sorry if that sounds uncharitable, but I can't get with any organisation that tells you never to walk alone in the hills.

By the time I cleared the slopes of Cairn Gorm I was thoroughly wet. The golf got no easier, the path here being a sliver of sand among thick heather. A young man whom I'd met at the Pools of Dee overtook me.

'You've got some great country here,' said David, a New Zealander. He had walked the jagged peaks of Skye during his three months in Britain but said he'd found the neatly plumped Cairngorms just as compelling. We stood and watched the rain clouds scudding across Rothiemurchus. 'Enjoy,' he said.

I followed the football – and occasionally a golf ball – down into the Caledonian forest where the trees crowded the path like over-enthusiastic fans, their branches catching the shallowest pitch, their roots pressing up through the hard soil like varicose veins so that even putting became erratic. Golf could only have taken off on the treeless coast, I thought . . .

Eventually the path opened out and I could take a full swing. It was still raining but muggy lower down, out of the breeze. I ran my hand along a footbridge railing, sweeping it clear of tepid water, a childish thrill. In all I had met 22 people in the expanse of the Lairig Ghru. Now I was running into families on mountain bikes and forest walkers on tea-time outings. One middle-aged couple had a vivacious young alsatian called Callie with them who couldn't decide whether he was scared of my orange football or wanted to chase it.

I spent the last mile walking the football through the trees, a very wearying way to finish after the dawn start. By then my Top Flites had long gone.

On reflection, the Lairig does share similarities with the Old Course. You play long and blind, your ball teased off-line by a capricious wind. It wasn't as gruelling to cross as the eastern slopes of Morven, nor as perturbing as Arthur Simmer's pig farm. What makes the Lairig so unforgiving, so unrelenting – whether you walk it or golf across it, is the fact that it stretches before you like a tightrope. You are hemmed-in by high mountains, boulders, precipitous burns, thigh-high heather and trees. You can't avoid these obstacles. They define the Lairig.

Most of the holes on the Old Course have a mat of rough before the fairway, some of them over 200 yards in length. Golfers go there to find out how good they really are. Most find out how bad they are. You are confronted by your limitations. Completing a round is as much a test of resolve as of golf.

I reached Coylumbridge after 1,442 shots – 15 rounds of golf compressed into a single day. My hands had stood up amazingly well; the skin had already hardened and thickened around the base of my fingers, on my left thumb, and in areas that stay soft when you're playing one round a week.

When it comes to withstanding the passage of walkers' boots, soil, alas, fails to develop a protective callous, like skin. A box on the edge of the estate contained a leaflet with a plea on behalf of the path:

Good to see you here, I hope you enjoy your visit

I reckon I've given enjoyment to tens of thousands of you over the years

Please continue to be kind to me and this very special countryside all around you

You can ensure I'm good for a few more years. A donation in the box will help.

The National Trust is spending one hundred thousand pounds repairing paths in the Cairngorms – not a sum that can be raised with a few strategically-placed piggy banks. The Rothiemurchus estate doesn't, however, depend entirely on donations. It also makes money through timber and tourism, off-road driving and clay-pigeon shooting. It welcomes visitors (both individuals and corporate groups), provides a map for mountain-bikers, and offers 'educational tours' that spotlight, among other things, land management and deer-farming. It isn't some jealously guarded national treasure or aristocratic indulgence.

Another leaflet in the box contained a greeting from the owner, John Grant, who described the estate as 'a wilderness garden, a place carefully nurtured over hundreds of years by the ancestors of families who still live and work here'. It turns out some 100 people. It was suggested a 'small camp in the remote hills for one night only should cause no problems, provided the site is left clean and tidy'. The Government already has a Concordant on Access which Rothiemurchus estate, among others, has signed up to. It urges:

> Freedom of access exercised with responsibility and subject to reasonable constraints for management and conservation purposes.

> Acceptance by visitors of the needs of land management, and understanding of how this sustains the livelihood, culture and community interests of those who live and work in the hills.

> Acceptance by land managers of the public's expectation of having access to the hills.

> Acknowledgment of a common interest in the natural beauty and special qualities of Scotland's hills, and of the need to work together for their protection and enhancement.

The Cairngorms have all sorts of international, national and regional designations associated with them. These include: 'Special Areas of Conservation', 'Special Protected Areas', 'National Nature Reserves', 'Sites of Scientific Interest', 'National Scenic Areas', 'Sites of Interest to Natural Science', 'Areas of Regional Landscape Significance', 'Environmentally Sensitive Areas' as well as three local nature reserves. When it comes to influencing development, these titles appear to have as much worth as a diploma you might buy on the internet. The voluntary agreements on land management drafted by quangos like Scottish Natural Heritage seem equally useless.

The real power lies with ownership. That's why the Scottish Parliament is planning to give communities the right to buy land as and when it comes up for sale. Some people are in a flap about Scotland being 'sold off' to foreigners, and suggest too much land is in too few hands. Perhaps they fear consortiums will buy up tracts of countryside, erect fences and turn-stiles, and levy entry fees. But these already exist in the form of parking charges, imposed by landowners, in places like Glen Tanar and Glen Clova where hillwalkers are happy to pay them, if only because they keep the masses away.

Scotland shapes up like a Monopoly board. Just 350 people own half the private land.

Andy Wightman, whose publications include *Who Owns Scotland?*, believes we stand at 'a remarkable and unprecedented moment in time' and has been advising the Scottish Parliament on its overhaul of our archaic land laws and feudal tenure system. He would like to see 'an agenda which brings together the essence of land reform – the redistribution of power — with the essence of modern politics – a progressive programme for building a better society'. Mr Wightman notes:

> In order to balance the public and the private interest there is a strong case for Parliament to legislate on providing a right to buy in alongside the creation of new fixed term tenancies. In other words there is a public interest in such matters which cannot be delegated to private parties to uphold – that is the job of Parliament.

Attempts at land reform have failed in the past, partly because those in power – the Lords, for example – have tended to be big landowners. However, I reckon land ownership is seen as something inviolable. It might make us feel uneasy that someone can call a mountain range their own, but I suspect the majority of Scots have been accepting of their role as serfs and vassals.

Mr Wightman wants to move the debate beyond big Highland estates and downtrodden crofters. He talks about the social democratic tradition of Western Europe where a place for community interest exists in the tenure system. In some countries the pattern of ownership is around 1,000 times less concentrated than in Scotland. Within these countries, community co-operatives own and run their own food processing and retailing operations, and do so with pride and enterprise. Mr Wightman is spot-on, surely, when he observes:

> . . . farmers in Scotland remain relatively powerless to control the linkages in their economic production systems because they do not own their own banks and supermarkets. Scotland's farming future lies in increased control of the processing and retail chain so that declining farm incomes can be compensated for by income from activities higher up the economic chain.

The community's right to buy land as and when it becomes available would be only a starting point for land reform. Other measures could include limiting the amount of land any one person can own, preventing estates being used as second-homes, and regulating the market, but the Parliament has yet to consider these.

It is proposing a 'right of responsible access for informal recreation', yet arguably the right to roam is already enshrined in Scottish law – the fact there is still no trespass. In the summer of 1999, Lord Reed, one of our youngest judges, stressed that Scotland is 'not a country where everything is forbidden except that which is expressly permitted. It is a country where everything is permitted except what is expressly forbidden.'

By and large big landowners don't get in the way of the nation's wanderlust. They might request that on certain days certain corries are avoided during the stalking season, but for much of the year you can walk and camp unhindered. I wonder if politicians and land-reformers would prove so sanguine if someone set up a tent in their back garden and shit in the roses?

As for the Cairngorms' forthcoming National Park status, this is what Stuart Black of the Cairngorms Partnership – set up by the Scottish Secretary in 1994 to coordinate debate on the mountains – told a Rural Affairs Committee in May 2000:

> Local people do not see their homeland as some sort of problem in need of a national park solution. They certainly do not want a national park that is there just for the sake of it so that people can say that Scotland has national parks. They do not want extra restrictions beyond those in the present designations. Instead, the people see this as an exciting opportunity to foster and build on the success that has already been achieved . . .

I've got a better idea: Time Share Mountains. The Government should buy up every Highland estate and offer people the chance to *own* the mountain of their dreams. That would stop them dropping litter. Over 60,000 people take to the Scottish hills each weekend during summer, many of them in gear costing hundreds of pounds, so the money is out there . . . People could roam wherever they wanted, as long as they keep to the official route – which would be marked with attractive fluorescent tape. Photographs of the summit view would be included in the price, should it be misty. Scottish mountains come in all shapes and sizes and there would be hundreds to choose from. People could even swap mountains with other members of Time Share Mountains. Anyone attending a viewing could be entered in a fabulous lucky draw for a gold-plated ice-axe, solid silver crampons or a plastic whistle.

**STROKES: 1442      TOTAL: 6020      SCORE: -138**

## *Golfing Holidays*

Courses abroad make you feel like a professional straight-off. The combination of sunshine, snakes and nitrate-saturated fairways always evokes Augusta. The backdrop may be inspiring but sadly handicaps rarely improve with the weather. If you want to revel in the Augusta illusion, don't shatter it by teeing off. Instead, grab a golf cart and ride around the course like Noddy. That's what everybody talks about anyway when they get home, the electric golf cart, not how they played. When you play abroad you are buying blue sky. Many courses in Spain and Portugal are technically and aesthetically inferior to those in Scotland, but are not places you might perish in during the winter. Golf tends to be more relaxing when you start your round with a few cold beers rather than a plate of soup. You will return home vowing to go back – and with a sense of astonishment that the game ever took hold over here.

# FOURTEEN

# One Man and Some Wolves

| HOLE 14 | DISTANCE: 13 | PAR: 812 |
|---------|--------------|----------|

'A downmarket resort in the Rockies that can't quite reinvent itself in the swanky image to which it aspires.'

'A shabby assortment of cavernous concrete buildings.'

THESE ARE TWO choice descriptions of Aviemore to be found in fashionable guidebooks. Few places in Scotland have had so much muck thrown at them over the years. You'd be forgiven for thinking the entire town was made of cardboard.

Thirty years ago it was given a new heart – a custom-made shopping and leisure centre. Unfortunately this transplant was rejected. Instead I found here boarded-up buildings, flaking paint, blacked out windows, bare earth, a weed-strewn dry ski-slope too short to fall down and a laughably big car-park. Only the go-karts remain, the track layout unchanged, the thrill undiluted for children and adults alike. Otherwise, the crazy golf, the ice-rink, the shops – all have been razed.

Redevelopment has stalled over the years as successive owners have tried to secure European grants. But now there's fifty million pounds in the kitty and there's a promise that work – including the building of an 18-hole golf course – will start soon.

This time around they are calling it a *Highland* resort rather than a mountain one – a sensible move. The Cairngorms are 12 miles away and have always been too flat to lend Aviemore any grandeur. The town lies at only 600 feet. In winter you don't walk upon the squeaky, dry snow of Continental resorts, but wade through dirty brown slush.

107

Like the farmers I met previously, people here are discovering that marketing is all-important. There needs to be more innovation. Walking could perhaps be repackaged as the ancient Nordic art of 'spasere' (to go for a walk). Glenmore Lodge could run courses in 'Historic Rambling': *Have you ever wondered what it would be like to walk in tweeds, climb with an axe made from hickory and a rope made from hemp?* 'The Ultimate Mountain Adventure' could involve getting lost, falling down a gully, and being rescued. How about 'Ski Bungi'? *Tackle the steepest slopes in perfect safety. No need to queue for a tow.*

Of course many tourists are too busy or too slothful to go traipsing up the Cairngorms, or to make the long and difficult walk across the car park to the chairlift. They tend to need to be offered some kind of mountain experience that doesn't involve mountains. To this end, the Aviemore Centre could be turned into a replica of the Cairn Gorm summit plateau – bleak, windswept and full of rocks. It's halfway there. It could be more rewarding than the real thing, given that funicular users will have all the freedom of school kids on a trip. The new owners should probably start filling out a Lottery funding application now:

> The Aviemore Interactive Mountain Centre
> Bringing solitude to YOU
> Shop and dine among the scenic splendour of the Cairngorms
> Go-karting still available

After breakfasting at a service station, I crossed the A9 and picked up an old road hidden among trees south of Lynwilg. The first few hundred yards were matted with moss and it was possible to pitch with a nine-iron, but I did so carefully. A hooked ball would have landed on the A9, a drag-strip running between Perth and Inverness. One driver was clocked at 155 mph on this road. The closing speed for any impact between golf ball and car could, then, be as high as 200 mph. That would certainly leave a dent.

The rain hadn't lifted but I didn't mind putting beneath dripping, sweet-smelling chestnut trees. A young welder was at work in his garage where the lights were on and the radio was playing. I asked about the weather forecast.

'It's going to rain all fucking day,' he said.

No ambiguity there, then. If only Michael Fish delivered the forecast with such unabashed confidence instead of muttering away about the pollen count and air quality. Just what are you supposed to do when the air quality forecast is bad? Stay indoors and not breathe?

The Lairig had eroded my lead over Scotland. It was a triple bogey – a derailment. I was now 138 under par, the equivalent of one-under on a normal round. As the Lairig had shown, that advantage could be squandered in five miles and there were still more than 60 to go. It was time to bring out my driver.

There was a field immediately after the garage, short grass, free of livestock. Using the number one wood I crossed it in three shots – a third of a mile. I followed a road through a farm, where a paddling pool hung out to dry in the tipping rain. The heather beyond was short enough to drive from. Four red deer staggered off up the hillside – heavy, unkempt beasts, like roe deer gone to hell with drink. After 88 shots I reached a wood where fox-gloves grew. The lower petals had been shed from the tall stems. They looked like golf flags.

What followed was a frustrating mix of perfect driving country and puddle-covered tracks that I could only putt on.

The route rose and fell across the arable hem of the Monadhliath Mountains. I was turned one way and then the other, as though the range was trying to flick some minor irritant from its skin. At one stage I became marooned in a field of cabbages and weeds, avoiding a penalty only by playing between hillocks which rose like skerries around me.

'Are you golfing across Scotland?' a man in a holiday home asked.

'Yes,' I replied flatly. There wasn't much more to say.

Between Alvie Lodge and Kincraig House the grass was again short and I had the fields to myself. For a mile I could strike the ball without restraint, but elected to play a percentage game. Rather than driving to within a few feet of a wall, and be forced to pitch over it, I'd play slightly short and use the wood again. Don't get me wrong. I wasn't standing among the sheep shit working out the yardage, tossing grass into the wind to divine its direction, painfully mulling over my club selection. I was simply hitting the ball well enough to plan a shot ahead. My swing wasn't yet a fluid, unthinking mechanical movement, but is was getting there.

Bales of hay lay around one field like giant bottle-corks. In this state, hay can actually be as dangerous as the animals that eat it. A Deeside farmer was crushed to death in 2000 when he tried to stop a bale rolling down a hillside.

My 248th shot carried me through a strand of wood. Beyond the trees

# PAR 10,000

I could hear whistling and garbled hollering. At Leault Farm a dozen tourists watched shepherd Neil Ross put his dogs through their paces. Ten border collies circled the sheep, bellies to the ground, their darkest instincts brought to the boil.

'Ops-ad-a-shed-up,' he cried. 'Come here you little bugger! Adia-abe-gap . . . Are you listening, Jim?!'

This perplexing combination of 'fast Scottish and Gaelic' helped Neil win BBC's *One Man and His Dog* in 1996. Like Tiger Woods' father, Neil believes you can train a champion.

'All these dogs will be good because they've been brought up to be good,' he said of the puppies flopping around our feet. 'If you bring a dog up to be mad it will be mad.'

At just four weeks the collies were all biddable. A fluttering of Neil's whistle soon brought them rushing for their porridge. In two years they would be ready to round up sheep.

Neil farms over 12,000 acres of heather moor that stretches 12 miles into the Monadhliath Mountains. He manages the sheep, but doesn't own them. It takes 7 men with 35 dogs 5 days to bring in all 2,500 of the flock. The rams are kept on the farm permanently so the birth of the lambs can be timed for April when the worst of the winter weather has usually passed.

Three pet lambs here mixed freely with the pack, sharing their bottled milk with the puppies. The day before they had been savaged by a rogue dog. Fist-sized chunks of flesh had been torn from their hindquarters and tails.

'We treated them immediately with antiseptic and penicillin,' said Neil. 'Otherwise they would have died.'

Neil didn't want to see the lurcher-cross ('a fine dog') destroyed, but was expecting the owner to pick up the vet's bills. 'Otherwise the dog will go to the warden.'

And so it was I found myself shearing a Scottish Black Face by hand, its head held firm between Neil's legs. Electric shears aren't used after July because they leave too little wool for winter. Sheep can't grow their coats when there's snow on the ground and no grass to eat.

As for the fleece, it was bound for Belgium, Italy or China to be made into 'the finest carpets in the world'. Neil said it would fetch fifty pence – what it cost him to shear the sheep. Dead, the animal wasn't worth much more.

'Last year a sheep sold for forty pounds,' he explained. 'Now it's worth between fifty pence and a fiver. The auctioneer takes one pound twenty, the haulier takes another one pound twenty.' Buyers, the ones who turn the sheep into meat, were paying rock-bottom prices after the BSE-bitten Government ruled that the spinal column should be removed at the abattoir. As a result the cost of slaughter jumped from five pounds to twenty-two pounds per animal.

Europe still produces only 80 per cent of the mutton it eats, yet the support paid to farmers (half of it by our own Government) isn't enough to provide an acceptable standard of living.

'Everybody's hanging on,' said Neil. 'Everybody's so much in debt. You keep waiting for the market to come back. All you know is farming.' Supermarkets were selling the component parts of the carcass for two hundred and twenty pounds, just as they had done the year before, but then they'd argue glitzy presentation and 24-hour shopping has its price. Neil could only repeat the farmers' angry refrain: 'Somebody's getting rich.'

At the end of the session, Neil set up a stall with whistles and postcards and badges, spread out on an old jacket in the farmyard.

He probably makes more from demonstrating how to do his job than from the job itself, which is sad. Sheep farming is supposed to be a working way of life but it could soon become an anachronism. Neil Ross could yet find himself in the Highland Folk Museum at Kingussie alongside spinners, weavers, dykers, rope-makers, and other craftsmen in quaint historical garb. But unlike, say, butter-making, it isn't mechanisation that is threatening to kill off sheep farming. It remains a labour-intensive industry, totally dependent on the skills of men and dogs. There's no cheap way to round up 2,500 sheep.

From Leault Farm I followed a path to the edge of the A9 before swinging back towards the mountains. In deference to some sheep I used a short-iron rather than the driver, but they soon cleared a fairway for me.

The hills ahead were steep and craggy. I turned south towards the 270-acre Highland Wildlife Park at Kincraig, home to wolves, lynxes, wild boar and other more immovable obstacles. A track shown on the map lay behind the perimeter fence which wasn't marked. Cars circled slowly among bison and what that looked like antelope, their passengers cocooned by glass and steel.

The Highland Wildlife Park was set up in 1972 and is run by the Royal Zoological Society of Scotland. Many of the animals and birds, you find on visiting, are housed within separate enclosures. Some come from 'broken homes'. Others have been injured beyond rehabilitation.

Surveys show the wolf is by far the most popular resident but centuries of vilification have left an indelible mark upon our collective psyche.

'What would happen if it got over the fence?' an awestruck youngster asked her mother as we watched the wolf pack trotting camply around their enclosure. To a little girl this is an animal that will eat your grandmother and don her still-warm cardigan, or blow your house down should you refuse it entry. Many of the qualities we admire in domestic dogs – their loyalty, communality, sense of hierarchy, big fluffy coats – come from the wolf. They are also beneficent creatures. If two wolves get into a scrap and one rolls over, exposing its belly, this submissive gesture ends the onslaught. I'll bet Neil Ross could get them to round up sheep.

But there have been bigger stars than the wolf at Kincraig. The advert for Famous Grouse Whisky was filmed here, but only after protracted negotiations. The advertising agency acting for United Distillers had asked if a cock red grouse could 'come into the studio'. Park manager Jeremy Usher-Smith said no.

'As grouse are very prone to stress,' he explained, 'we could not agree to this, so the only option was to move the photographer and his studio into the aviary.' The park wanted 'full control of the whole process' and would only work with a professional wildlife photographer who understood 'the needs of the bird'. They got the lot.

A white background was essential. To help the birds acclimatise, a white door was laid on the aviary floor, covered with turf and heather that was removed gradually over a period of days. One nameless bird 'took to this with grace'. On the day of the shoot, Jeremy explained, he 'went to work like an old professional' and lacked only the gumption to demand his own trailer and to tie up a share of the profits and merchandising rights. Stardom never went to his head, though, and the grouse remained in the aviary with his friends (presumably because the gate was shut) until his death a few years ago at seven years of age.

When pushed to name his favourite animal, Jeremy nods in the direction of the pine marten. With its bewitching, black eyes, lustrous brown coat, and creamy chest fringed with ginger, it's an oriental cat bred to the point of abstraction. Cute, yes, but not for stroking. This is the weasel of the trees. Lunch can be a squirrel, which says something about its athleticism.

'It has the dexterity of a concert pianist,' said Jeremy. 'It's like a small primate.' Pine martens are among Scotland's rarest animals but locals haven't always welcomed the park's attempt to breed them, one person describing them to Jeremy as 'disgusting vermin'.

'Come to the Highland Wildlife Park and see Scotland's disgusting vermin . . .' Doesn't have quite the same appeal, does it?

The park's grand plan isn't just to boost wildlife numbers, but to reintroduce species like the beaver to Scotland. The habitat needs to be there first, though, and that means educating landowners.

'Many manage the land the same way it was managed in Victorian times,' said Jeremy. 'It's based around stalking, grouse and fishing.' If native woodland was allowed to grow back it could support wild boar (which would be just as much fun to shoot as stag and would look more impressive mounted on the lounge wall). This in turn would pave the way for the bigger predators.

'The difficult one will be the bear,' said Jeremy, half-joking. 'The problem with rearing and releasing a bear is that they can associate humans with food.'

As someone who has raised a chaffinch in his bedroom, I know what Jeremy means.

This bird's mother was killed on the nest, along with the rest of the brood, by a cat. I thought it would refuse to take food – but it accepted bread soaked in water and minced worms. Its feathers grew and after a few weeks I let it go, launching it into the air in the back garden. Twenty minutes later another neighbour turned up at the door with the bird. It had landed on someone's head on the disused railway line where she had been walking her dog. I hadn't stopped to think the chaffinch might associate all humans with me, and therefore show them no fear.

'Chirps', as the bird was named, lived with my aunt Sheila for 14 years and had 'free-fly' of her house. A chaffinch might perhaps lack the charisma of a bear, but this mundane, ubiquitous garden bird was fascinating at close-range – the way she sheared the wings off a fly before swallowing it, picked food from your tongue and fanned herself on a lamp-shade above the warmth of the bulb. Her green-brown plumage proved to be a stippling of many colours.

Appreciate what you have – that's the ethos behind the Highland Wildlife Park. It encourages us to admire animals and birds found on both sides of the perimeter fence.

Eco-tourism can work. The nearby Insh Marshes Reserve is formed by 1,000 hectares of wetland on the floodplain of the River Spey between Kingussie and Kincraig. It is home to rare birds and plants.

In summer the marshes are grazed by sheep and cattle and this allows the other plants to flourish and keeps willows at bay. Both the Royal Society for Protection of Birds and the farmers benefit. So does the local community, and not just from the cash 10,000 visitors bring. The floodplain also keeps the Spey from bursting its banks elsewhere.

To continue westwards I had to climb another high fence. I couldn't be sure I wasn't entering some far-flung pen, but the presence of a lone sheep, calmly scoffing grass, suggested this was still hillside.

The wood ahead – a thatch of fern, birch and prickly juniper – was too matted for golf. Using an iron as a machete, and locked onto a compass bearing, I ducked and scrambled my way over the slippery, broken, rasping ground to reach a path quarter of a mile away. My penalty: a skinned shin and 50 strokes.

I continued towards Balavil, a grand country house with a sea-faring crest high above its door. It was still raining, the drops thick, warm, sub-tropical. I managed to lose a tennis ball among some nettles and put another down the steep side of a burn. It emerged on the other bank, in the middle of a tree-felling operation. Chainsaws – now *there's* a noise to put you off your putt.

Again I was able to find my way into a field and use the driver. My final approach to Kingussie converged with the A9. The last few hundred yards involved crossing a marshy field of young birch trees and reedy grass. I stepped over a fence to join the road near the Kingussie turn-off. It had taken eight hours to come thirteen miles.

When you're golfing across moorland it can be hard to judge how your game is coming along. I was certainly hitting the ball better. The fluffs had diminished; the accuracy had improved. A vehicle track was now an easy target with any club shorter than a seven-iron. Playing football with a grapefruit had improved the young Pele's skills. Playing golf with a football had hopefully done the same for mine . . .

The test came at Kingussie Golf Club. Secretary Norman MacWilliam welcomed me to the course, which unfolds among birch, alder and pine on a knobbly hillside above the town. Its designer was Harry Vardon, Britain's best golfer at the turn of the twentieth century and a winner of championships on both sides of the Atlantic.

'He had a real eye for it,' said Norman.

I thought Jack Nicklaus was the first pro to launch his own line in golf courses. Norman was appalled. 'Have you never heard of Donald Ross from Dornoch?! He had a hand in hundreds of American courses.'

# ONE MAN AND SOME WOLVES

Kingussie is not one man's vision imposed on the land, but something more subtle and empathetic. Varden worked with nature rather than bending it to his will. 'Nicklaus designs courses for a certain type of golf,' said Norman. 'They've got the machines now . . .'

The club was formally opened on 10 July 1891. The *Inverness Courier* reported that 'the first ball was hit off in good style by Miss Bryce Smith, of Manchester, amid cheers'. I did less well.

The tee is in full view of the clubhouse. In times of pressure you revert to what you know. My drive was a woeful compromise between my old swashbuckling swing (all arms) and the tighter, athletic one I'd been practising in the mountains.

The ball veered left and dived into some rough at the edge of the par-three's green. I thinned the pitch, took five.

A golf course is no place for panic. If Tiger Woods has made tournaments dull, it is because he has turned golf into a game of attrition. During this year's Open he was content to shoot par over the first nine holes, knowing that the spectacular early leaders would soon break down. I tried to relax, to picture heather rather the flag. After a shaky first four holes – which included a seven and an eight – I settled down and made three pars before the turn.

On the inward nine the two players in front asked if I wanted to join them. Bernard Fletcher, a retired bank manager from Yorkshire, was on holiday with his son, Matthew. He had played Kingussie in May. 'It's wonderful up here,' he said. 'You're away from everything.'

The Fletchers and I chatted about walking in the Cairngorms, getting lost in the Cairngorms, Matthew's geology dissertation, jobs, increasing workloads and early retirement. The golf seemed secondary, although a silence ensued whenever someone addressed their ball. During a round you spend about two and half minutes swinging the club; it's daft to get too hung up on the outcome . . .

The *Book of Kingussie*, published in 1911, carries a poem by Rev. John Smith which rejoices in the sight, sounds and smells awaiting those who take to the course:

> Come, all ye gay golfers – here's luck to your name! –
> Come, shoulder your clubs, ye that love the old game.
> And come, I will lead you to Gynack's green glen,
> Far away from the haunts and business of men.

# PAR 10,000

Oh, come when the dew-drop lies thick on the grass,
When the mist like a shroud hides the dark mountain pass,
When the first woodland praise to high Heaven is borne,
And the resinous pine scents the breath of the morn.

But first pause on the brae-top adjoining the Mill,
And dwell on the splendour of wood, vale and hill;
While the murmuring stream, as it gurgles along
With a leap and a dance, soothes the ear with its song . . .

Oh, come with your 'swallow', your 'hawk', or your 'kite';
Let your 'rubber-core' soar unrestrained in its flight.
Avoid the dread bunker, the hazard, and still
Here you'll find just the course that will test your best skill.

Come, then, for a space; leave the hot, dusty street.
At Kingussie a good Highland welcome you'll meet.
There is life, there is health, there's romance in the air
Of the Queen of all golf links, Glen Gynack the fair!

I came back in 40 for a total of 85 – a quantifiable improvement in my play.

While this performance was unlikely to earn a Ryder Cup call-up, it does demonstrate why Tiger Woods is last to leave the practice range; why, when he was a child, he used to hit balls until his arms chafed so badly they bled. He may play with a fancy set of clubs today, but that's a minor factor in his course-busting ability.

When Harry Vardon visited Kingussie in 1906 to make plans to extend the nine-hole course to eighteen holes, he played a demonstration match with J.S. Herd, using clubs no cleverer than an upturned walking stick. They completed two rounds over a course that was longer and much rougher than today's 18. Vardon shot 67.

**STROKES: 508     TOTAL: 6528     SCORE: -442**

# The Ryder Cup

The biennial Ryder Cup is golf's attempt to turn what is emphatically an individual sport into a team game. It was first fought between the United States and Britain in 1927 but after 52 years the Brits realised they were no damned good and grudgingly decided to let the rest of Europe join their team. Just 14 years later they won – the first victory in 28 years. One of Britain's most cherished results came at Royal Birkdale in 1969. The team drew brilliantly after a charitable Jack Nicklaus, under the rules of match play, invited Tony Jacklin to knock his ball away rather than tackle a tricky putt. The steely Jacklin didn't miss. The Ryder Cup finally came of age as a team event in 1999, when spectators started drinking in the stands and swearing at players.

## FIFTEEN

# General Wade's Golf Course

| HOLE 15 | DISTANCE: 13 MILES | PAR: 812 |
| --- | --- | --- |

THE HOTEL OWNER came at me brandishing a knife.

'Don't worry, I'm not going to murder you,' she said. 'This is just for making my apple pie.' Aileen Burrow stood laughing in the entrance to the Osprey Hotel.

She and her husband Norman had moved to Kingussie from Yorkshire, and had bought the hotel during a recession. She described living in Scotland as 'going back ten years in time'. At first I thought she was talking about our crumbling roads and infrastructure, but it was the purity of the air and the absence of traffic jams she'd meant.

I rose early the next day. Dalwhinnie is a day's walk from Kingussie and I was aiming to catch a late-afternoon train back to the hotel. After breakfast (moist scrambled eggs, a slab of smoked haddock, sweet mushrooms, homemade bread) I putted my way out of the town, over the River Spey.

Ruthven Barracks lies to the left of here. It sits trophy-like upon a mound of grass at the junction of three roads built by General George Wade, who was Commander in Chief of North Britain from 1724–40. He was employed by King George I to smash the Highland clan system following the first Jacobite uprising of 1715. Wade needed to mobilise his soldiers and built 240 miles of roads and 40 bridges. Ruthven, one of four Highland garrisons, housed 120 redcoats and also the dragoons who patrolled these roads on horseback. The barracks were torched in 1746 by Bonnie Prince Charlie's army during their retreat from Prestonpans – a last defiant gesture before their annihilation at Culloden.

One of Wade's roads cuts straight through the hills from Ruthven to Etteridge, six miles to the south west. The first mile appears to have been appropriated by the makers of the A9 and I had to make a diversion through a field, an alleyway of pine trees and across some boggy heather.

Wade's road is a gift for the golfer. It is flat, straight, open and carpeted with grass. Although I didn't expect to meet many people on this route, it would have been remiss to drive over the few blind crests. A Top Flite XL Super Range ball leaves my club at around 80 mph. That turns a driver into a musket. It would have been quite possible to split someone's head open. A few years ago a 46-year-old accountant lost nine teeth and part of his gum after being hit by a golf ball. He was in hospital for six weeks. A woman lost an eye on a course outside Aberdeen after her ball rebounded off a rock lying in some long grass. I didn't want to become a latter-day dragoon, bringing down ordinary Scots as they walked their land.

The 56th shot brought me to a burn that was bigger than the map suggested. After wading across it I sat on the bank and dried my feet, scanning the denuded mountain slopes, thinking how drab the mosaic of new and old heather looked under the gathering cloud. In Scotland we cleared the hills of trees, firstly for grazing and then crop production. Deer were left to feed on the few remaining seedlings so they might multiply and satisfy the bloodlust of the gentry. In the nineteenth century great areas of land were turned into sporting estates and communities were once again marginalised.

Yet we still have the gall to criticise countries like Brazil for chopping down the rainforest, making native people homeless and hastening global warming. We forget that our own companies share in the profits from the timber and the space created for farming and building. We expect Brazil to leave its trees standing to absorb the carbon dioxide belching forth from our factories and cars. Brazil should start exporting the oxygen generated by the rainforests. That would reduce its international debt. You've got the bomb; we've got the rainforest.

It's going to be years before there's irrefutable evidence of global warming (at least ten) so perhaps we shouldn't start panicking just yet. True, glaciers in Antarctica have started to dribble away, but fears that rising sea levels could play havoc with the Munro tables are unfounded; Scotland is still springing back after being weighed down by glaciers during the last Ice Age. If we're smart enough to have created a problem like global warming, I'm sure we're smart enough to get it sorted out . . .

I crossed a humped-back bridge. It looked like a hand-crafted Wade original. There was a small patch of cement underneath it, but one filling in 250 years isn't bad.

A small toad sat unblinking on the path. The skin on its right hind leg had split at the joint to reveal dull pink flesh underneath. I gently prodded the toad, expecting it to flip over and reveal a belly festooned with maggots, but its body was soft, heavy and inflated. The animal was certain to dry out in the sun so I placed it in a ditch, hoping to ease any suffering (although I might have prolonged it).

I remember at school one of my teachers warned the class that if we ever found him screaming his life away in a car wreck we must prevent paramedics from administering morphine. To suffer is to be human – or at the very least a toad. The teacher, one of the most popular at the school, eventually committed suicide.

Losing balls was now part of my plan. (I wanted to shed the majority before I reached Etteridge, get myself down to landing weight for the putt-jog along the old A9 to Dalwhinnie.) It was almost disappointing to find them on the path.

# PAR 10,000

Away from the golf course I'd stopped flapping my arms like a penguin. Twisting my torso generated more power and cured my habitual slice. Most of my drives were long and straight although there was still a tendency to aim left, which left the ball in the heather. Poor players tend to compensate in this way rather than addressing the rudimentary flaws in their game. I had once mistaken my banana-shot off the tee for idiosyncratic brilliance.

I entered a short stretch of birch wood using the putter and a nine-iron. A goldcrest, no bigger than a golf ball, oscillated between the branches. Partridges were everywhere, rushing around with a gangling, teetering stride, never quite reaching take-off velocity. The birds I saw had been bred in cages to be shot. The adults are released and enticed to hang around the estate with free feed. It's Death Row disguised as Paradise.

Some sporting estates have a deer sanctuary, a corrie where no hunting ever takes place. The animals feel secure there and so remain on the land – although clearly they might take a bullet in the brain the moment they step outside. A refuge can quickly become a prison.

On the right of the wood was a small loch. Two boats were being rowed noisily back and forth, the occupants chatting, guffawing and fishing. They were probably the laird's family or friends – not serious anglers judging by the din. I sat on the bank where a spaniel and labrador were pacing, watching for a bit.

'Got one,' said a woman. The fly rod bent double. I'd thought small lochs had been all but emptied of fish and I expected her to land some weed or, if she was lucky, a branch.

'Oh my god it's big.' The trout's bronze underbelly brushed the surface, the fish disappearing with a tight splash. She will have felt its tremulous power, amplified by the rod – a sensation George Orwell described as the most exciting of his adult life.

'Beauty,' said one of the men. The reel shed some line as the fish ran with it.

'Don't do anything jerky,' advised the other woman in the boat.

Five minutes later the weary fish was drawn towards the keel.

'Oh my God it's big,' the woman repeated. 'Holy shit!'

The fish was lifted from the water in a net: a brown trout, maybe four pounds. While one of the men grappled with the fish, burning its flesh with his dry hands as he tried to remove the fly from its mouth, a debate ensued about whether or not to keep it.

'We don't have a camera,' someone shouted from the other boat, vanity sealing the trout's fate. The man walloped its head repeatedly off the seat. From the bank it looked as though he was trying to throttle it.

I wanted to shout 'throw it back'. Catching a fish is arguably sport – persuading it to take the fly; landing it on a light line. Killing one, however, can only be an unequal struggle. After all, when it comes to mortal combat, fish are distinctly disadvantaged out of water. A great white shark would never make the first-round bell in a boxing match.

If fish are handled correctly, I don't think they're any worse-off on being returned to the water (too sore in the gum to ever eat again, that sort of thing). When I was a kid I put a trout back with a hook still in its mouth. I caught the same fish two minutes later, removed the first hook and left the second. These days I use a hook without a barb. Maybe one day I'll fish with nothing on the end of the line. This might be the sustainable future of Britain's most popular hobby.

The ground beyond the wood was so like a fairway I found myself on the verge of replacing divots. I putted my way along a vehicle track beyond the estate lodge and reached a croft beside the A9 after just over 200 shots. The plan was to putt along the old A9 for six miles to Dalwhinnie. I decided to hide the rest of the clubs in a bush and collect them in the car.

'You could leave them in the porch,' said the woman at the croft.

Two minutes later I was relaxing in the home of Isobel MacBean, with coffee on its way.

Isobel's husband John, who had just celebrated his 80th birthday, came south from Ross-shire as a young man to find work and ended up spending nearly 40 years as farm manager on the estate I had just crossed. When John retired the couple were allowed to remain in the estate cottage which for so many years had been their home.

'Not many estates do that,' said Isobel.

She was also given 'a few sheep' which she keeps as pets along with some chickens and a 'bissom' of a duck that had led 11 chicks to an early death that summer, just short of the water that would have kept them safe from predators like foxes. 'It was too far. They weren't able to get there. They fell over and died.'

The coffee arrived with a scone, a pancake and a rock cake – a Holy Trinity of pieces. Isobel refused to sit down or feed herself, preferring instead to chivvy the world along. She was flabbergasted to hear I had paid thirty two pounds for bed-and-breakfast at the Osprey Hotel, but glad I hadn't used a credit card.

'People say that if they didn't have credit cards they would have nothing. These days they want more and more money.' Isobel was proud that, like her mother, she had 'never had a flitting . . . not many people can say that.'

Contentment surely isn't measured by what you achieve, but by the gap between that and what you strive for.

Today's generation isn't greedy; we're just choking on aspiration. One TV will do, but it must be digital, with Dolby Pro-Logic Surround-Sound, a 70-inch flat screen and whatever else is new. And there must be thousands of fathers pushing their infant sons to play golf well so that they, the fathers, might avenge their own inadequacies – and maybe, just maybe, produce the next Tiger Woods. There can be only one top dog, however, which leaves the majority feeling chronically embittered.

If we hoped for less we might well be happier, but then we would still be living in caves. The desire to show off – to prevail – has taken us far. In the rush to prosper we are falling over ourselves. We build houses on the edge of towns to provide homes for those who move there to work in the construction trade. The bigger the harvest of cheap GM food there is to go round, the more hungry mouths there will be to meet it.

'I'll try and get the rest of your clubs sold before you come back,' said Isobel as I picked up the putter to leave.

'Well, make sure you get a good price,' I said.

THE old A9 is part of the National Cycle Network. I expected a cute little road within a road, complete with benches and bins, but no. The Government seems to have spent millions of pounds *signposting* existing roads on the network when any cyclist with elementary map-reading skills can figure out how to avoid dual carriageways and trunk roads.

Bikes have become part of the Government's vision of transport in the twenty-first century: everybody pedalling to work, those better-off in rickshaws. The fact that you're fifteen times more likely to die on a bike is something politicians tend to keep quiet when promoting cycling.

As is the case with a lot of the network, you still share the old A9 with some cars. Because the road is so quiet, some of them are driven at high speed, which added a frisson to my golf. It's bad enough on a bike when you have buses and lorries bearing down on you, squealing and steaming like mechanical bulls, threatening to turf you into the path of on-coming vehicles. Vigilance and rapid reactions are necessary for survival here. I must have looked pretty shifty – constantly peering over my shoulder, sprinting away from cars, snatching some object from the ground, diving into bushes . . .

The 321st shot rolled to halt in the remains of a rabbit and was held fast by slimy fur and splintered bone. I knocked the tennis ball away into the heather and took a second from the waistcoat – a true professional.

As I arrived in Dalwhinnie, two RAF Tornado jets corkscrewed overhead, rumbling and crackling as they went, like God clearing his throat. The noise alone would prompt any flaky ground-based enemy army to lay down its weapons. Shortly afterwards, an old American fighter plane chugged across the sky with a pleasingly mechanical rhythm, possibly on its way to an air-show.

I'd come over 100 miles and hadn't seen one golden eagle. So much for it being king of the skies.

Dalwhinnie lies at over 1,000 feet. The name comes from the Gaelic word 'dilcoinneeamb', meaning 'plain of meetings'. Eighteenth-century cattle drovers would replenish themselves in the village on the way to the markets in Crieff and Falkirk.

Bonnie Prince Charlie spent a fortnight on the shores of nearby Loch Ericht after his challenge for the throne collapsed at Culloden. Field-Marshall Montgomery also stayed here during the height of World War Two, fishing by day and plotting the D-Day landings at night – and Queen Victoria arrived here incognito with her husband, Prince Albert. She complained later in her diary of being served 'two miserable starved Highland chickens' at an inn. I wonder if Victoria sometimes adopted a silly voice during these secret trips.

('The name's eh . . . Mrs. . . Mrs Queen. And this is my husband, Mr Queen . . .') I assume she remembered to remove her crown.

Dalwhinnie's whisky distillery is the highest in Scotland. I joined a party of visitors a few minutes into the tour here, quietly taking my place at the back. The guide clocked me and recapped on her introduction.

'We use barley, water and yeast to make whisky,' she said. 'The water comes from the loch behind the distillery and the barley comes from a place called M-o-r-a-y-s-h-i-r-e.' I nodded slowly. She obviously thought I was foreign.

Up until the late nineteenth century, brandy had been the country's favourite tipple. When disease rampaged through European vineyards, glasses emptied of wine and attention turned to whisky. Three Speyside men raised ten thousand pounds to build the distillery here in 1897.

Within months of starting production it went into liquidation. In 1905 the United States' biggest distiller bought it over, prompting familiar fears that the entire industry would fall into foreign hands, (able and nurturing though they might have been). Prohibition saved the day though, and the distillery was sold back to Scottish owners.

The production process has changed little since then. The barley is soaked in water, allowed to germinate and then smoke-dried in a peat fire (the malting). At the distillery it is watered again, and starches break down into a sugary liquid known as 'wort'. Yeast turns this glorious-smelling effluent into crude alcohol. Distillation takes place in two huge copper cones; even the shape affects taste. The whisky – an annual 3.5 million litres – matures for 15 years in bourbon barrels that are imported and reassembled, to give it a distinctive flavour.

Marisa, the guide, explained all of this in English and repeated parts in her native Italian tongue. It was like being at the Eurovision Song Contest.

There was a nip waiting at the end of the tour. Whisky remains the most popular spirit in the world and is one of the UK's top five export earners. Around one in 50 Scottish jobs rely on the industry. Marisa warned us that whisky shouldn't be drunk with ice 'or they will shoot you'. I didn't dare ask about lemonade or Red Bull.

Like many Scots under 40, I prefer vodka to whisky. That is, I prefer the bland taste of the stuff you buy in supermarkets, which is easily dulled with a mixer. It's the same story in the United States. Nearer home, the European Union is considering introducing a minimum level of spirit duty that could decimate sales in places like Spain – the second biggest export market after the US.

Another threat to the industry was averted this summer when the EU agreed to exempt Scotland from a tax on water, intended to help protect supplies from improvident industrial users. The judgement about who does pay is being left to the Scottish Executive. It's hoped the bureaucracy associated with this new directive can be kept to a minimum.

Over 30 distilleries draw water from the River Spey and its tributaries, but not in any huge quantity. Power production uses more. Even with these demands the Spey is rarely bereft of water. It is among the least modified – and least polluted – large river systems in the UK and in recent years was described by the North East River Purification Board as almost 'pristine'. A new role for the farmer could perhaps involve planting riverside trees, creating fords, restoring floodplains and generally undoing the ham-fisted damage of the past.

# GENERAL WADE'S GOLF COURSE

The Dalwhinnie malt certainly sounded good: 'The pureness of the water imparts a soft, whispery taste . . . the gentle finish starts sweetly, then lingers on to yield a smoky, malty Highland glow . . . flavours dancing a brisk reel in the mouth.' It smelled not bad either, a splash of water bringing out its 'tight-knit' citrus aroma and 'honeyed sweetness'. (And yes, it tasted okay. I didn't wince once.)

Young Scots may yet take to their national drink. Shaking hands on meeting people, listening to Radio Four in the car, wearing flannels, smoking a pipe, contemplating joining a golf club, drinking whisky – at first you do these things with a sense of ironic detachment, but gradually you embrace them. The knowing smile evaporates, leaving the essence of the man or woman, usually not dissimilar to that of the parents. I expect that one day I will end up wearing my golf bonnet in the car as I drive along at 20 mph, crouched behind the wheel.

Dalwhinnie still feels like a frontier town, somewhere itinerants eke a living from the cold, implacable earth. Fifty years ago the winter snows used to pile to twenty feet. One distillery employee walked to work over the roofs of cars later to be retrieved in the spring thaw. It still manages to be one of the coldest places in Britain, the temperature averaging around 6 °C.

Though the hotel by the train station was up for sale, the curtains remained open and the stools by the bar awaited your backside. The parasols in the front porch were shut like flowers, ready to open when the conditions were right. The hotel had obviously learned to hibernate.

I found myself alone at the un-staffed station and sat and dangled my legs over the platform. The train arrived on time and tracked for two, maybe three miles straight across what felt like unbroken tundra, leaving behind a village of fleeting, almost lawless charm.

I finished the night in The Tipsy Laird in Kingussie, drinking Dalwhinnie. At 10 p.m. a guy called Steve Mac arrived with his karaoke unit. The place was full but nobody was volunteering to be the first. 'What the hell', I thought – karaoke in Kingussie was something to try. Steve didn't have any bothy ballads.

'I think I've taken out the Scottish disc,' he explained. 'The songs on it weren't that great.' He gave me a song-list. I was perusing it in the toilet when I got chatting to a member of a BBC film crew, in Scotland to make a second series of *Monarch of the Glen*.

'Any requests?' I asked.

'"Stairway to Heaven".'

'And your name is?'

'Do they have it?' He sounded surprised.

They did. '71A.'

Steve Mac had just finished singing 'Teddy Bear' and 'The Sweetest Thing' when I took the mike for this monolithic song.

It must be said that Led Zepellin doesn't really work with a drum-machine and a sequencer.

'Oh . . . oh-oh-oh,' went the prompt. And then came the guitar solo. Just what are you supposed to *do* at this point? Dance? Order another drink from the bar? In a desperate attempt to ingratiate myself with the crowd, I climaxed with: 'And she's buy-yee-ing a stairway . . . to Kingussie.' I may have even winked at them.

As I trundled up the road to the hotel it wasn't the voice of singer Robert Plant that echoed around my skull but Marisa's. Of the 'Gentle Spirit' she had warned: 'Sometimes people don't know what they've been drinking until afterwards.'

**STROKES: 421     TOTAL: 6949     SCORE: -833**

# *Keeping the Faith*

If I hadn't gone out of bounds at the first – and into the bunker at the second – and four-putted the third – and three-putted the fourth – and taken a five at the short fifth – and over-clubbed at the sixth – and under-clubbed at the seventh – and rushed, my putt on the eighth – and taken too long over my drive on the ninth . . . if I hadn't been held up at the tenth – and the eleventh – and been put off by the group that let me play through their chatting on the tee at the twelfth – and been so bold with my approach at the thirteenth – and too timid at the fourteenth . . . if I had kept my eye on the ball at the fifteenth – and hadn't sliced at the sixteenth – and hooked at the seventeenth – and if I'd managed to sneak an albatross at the last . . . I'd have broken ninety.

# SIXTEEN

# In a Rut

**HOLE 16       DISTANCE: 20 MILES       PAR: 1250**

THIRTY-FIVE MILES of mountain and moor lay ahead. Crossing it would require an overnight stay, and even then I'd have to trot between shots. A tent, stove, pans and other utilitarian items were too much of an encumbrance.

I thought about cooking over a real fire and sleeping out under the stars, as I've done many times before. I know that sounds a bit 'Tom Sawyer', but you do get a perfectly good sleep among the heather. The only discomfort I've experienced came when I woke late one summer morning with sunburn on one side of my face. A fire is always worth the effort too. A camping stove won't drive away midges or keep you warm throughout the night; there's no cheer in its frothy, blue flame.

I was just reaching for my sleeping bag and lighter when I looked again at the map. At the far end of Loch Ossian was a red triangle: a youth hostel. A trawl around the internet threw up a phone number for it. Yes, it was open. Yes, they had a bed. What's more, there was a kitchen, with pots, pans and cutlery and they had duvet covers . . . All I needed to bring was £6.75 and a sheet sleeping bag.

The hostel was well over halfway to Kinlochleven. Since I would be travelling light, I reckoned I could reach it just before darkness. At least a good night's sleep would be guaranteed.

At 6.30 a.m. I parked the car near Dalwhinnie station where I pulled on the waistcoat loaded up with 120 golf balls. My small rucksack contained:

# PAR 10,000

Two Maps
Compass
Kagoule
Waterproof trousers
Cap
Spare underwear
Torch
Freeze-dried food
Stub of soap
Toothbrush
British Airways-issue toothpaste
Sheet sleeping bag
60 golf balls

The other thing I always carry is a knife. (Well, you never know when you might need to clean your finger nails or sharpen a pencil.) It's a Swiss Army model, but not one of those that packs everything bar a lathe. Victorinox, the manufacturer, seems to have a gadget for every occasion, including a GolfTool that has a pitch repairer, a groove-cleaner-cum-tee-puncher (for frozen ground), and a ball marker with the company's logo. My knife isn't quite so manly as the *Huntsman*, the *Explorer*, the *Ranger* or the *Mountaineer*. It's a Swiss Army *Picnic*, bought some years ago. The nearest model available today is the Swiss Army *Waiter*.

A thin film of frost had settled on the land overnight. I sensed it in my hands and then underfoot as I kicked through the stiff grass, looking for the first pushed ball of the day. I switched to the tennis ball as I passed a gate-house where someone was settling down before a computer screen, and I side-stepped towards Loch Ericht when the track grew twisty.

The ball bounced among the pebbles but there was sand and tuft to play from. I cast a fifty-foot shadow as I strode along the sunlit shore. Within half an hour the chill had started to lift. Sunlight raked the corries of Ben Alder where shadows lingered in the folds of rock. The effect was that of a stage curtain being peeled back – a thrilling opening to the day. Ben Alder is described in the Scottish Mountaineering Club's guidebook as one of the country's 'great remote mountains', yet such is its size it seemed only a few miles away to me.

The soft earth track straightened; it provided good lies and cushioned the ball on landing. I carried a single club, a five iron, which could send the ball up to 140 yards. I tended only to take a half a swing, however. There were quite a few crests and vehicles, even this early in the day. It was possible to find the ball among the thin track-side vegetation and I made every effort to look: I expected to lose many balls in the heather beyond.

The turreted, fairytale Ben Alder Lodge pokes between pine trees four miles along the loch. Swiss financier Urs Schwarzenbach, whose company Agro Investment Overseas Ltd owns 75 per cent of the 26,000 acre Ben Alder estate, spent £9 million on it. With the approval of the Highland Council he diverted two rights of way in order to maintain its privacy, adding just over a quarter of a mile to a twelve-mile route from Dalwhinnie to a bothy. A planning officer reported:

> I am satisfied that the proposed diversion of the two routes which pass close to Ben Alder Lodge will act to enhance the amenity, security and privacy of the lodge and hence increase its letting and sale value. I consider that in all the circumstances diversion of the routes is expedient to secure efficient use of the land or of other land held therewith. I am satisfied that there is no detrimental impact upon a walker's enjoyment of the route.

This decision was based on the Countryside (Scotland) Act 1967. Its introduction was ostensibly about access, but predicated on the belief that trespass is a crime. More than 30 years on, Scottish Natural Heritage is pushing our parliament to legislate for a 'right of responsible access'. It too wants to spell out exceptions – hardly surprising when it sees trespass as a 'civil wrong' and insists 'most people on land are in the position of being trespassers'. When it comes to preserving liberty, the humble right of way – whether that's the Lairig Ghru or a short-cut to the shops – is something to be cherished.

I reached the gates of the lodge in 126 shots. The waistcoat had helped proportion nearly 20 pounds of golf balls about my body. A third were held in the big back pocket where they acted like ballast to keep my back straight, curing an inveterate stoop.

As I looked back towards Dalwhinnie I could scarcely credit how far I'd come in so few shots. I'd covered the distance of an 18-hole course yet had taken only 40 more than I might have on its tailored playing surface. But that is the story of amateur golf. You will carry the fairway of a 380-yard hole in two shots, then take three or four more to tidy the ball into the cup. I had found power and accuracy in the hills, but not the deft touch so crucial on and around the green.

The path forked right, away from the lodge and across stony ground where the tennis ball worked best. I paused at a junction to allow an estate vehicle to pass and followed the track onto open moor above the forest. The heather was scanty and I was able to play a proper ball from the grass verge, again choosing to hit it around 100 yards.

I was now in the heart of what the OS map describes as 'Ben Alder Forest', though the land is devoid of trees. Across its flat expanse, Ben Alder and Aonach Beag rear up like ocean liners in a harbour, their thrusting ridges filling the horizon. Some of the corries still held patches of old snow, which would last throughout the year. There is sometimes a fall in early autumn, the snow blowing in overnight. In Highland villages the precipitation falls as rain, hosing leaves from the trees and the memory of summery days from people's minds. The next morning is often still and bright and the snow lies like lace across the surrounding hills, its sudden appearance no less exciting than the accumulation of Christmas presents beneath a tree.

During the heatwave summer of 1976, the Grampians were blanketed as low as 1,600 feet after snow fell on 9 and 10 September. On the high tops it was as deep as three feet and provided a fortnight's skiing.

A few hundred yards to my left, two men waded through the heather, one with a rifle slung over his shoulder: the keeper and a client, out to shoot a stag. When the keeper trained his binoculars on me, I decided to let him know I'd cleared my route with the estate factor. As I bounded across the heather he moved to intercept, distancing the shooter from the disturbance. You don't charge a man thousands of pounds to go stalking on a golf course.

'I'll be keeping to low ground,' I said.

'No, not low ground, the *paths*.'

'Yes, paths.'

The keeper's tone was brusque, his body language uncompromising. Mind you, I understood his disquiet. This was in effect his office and there was every chance I would end up scattering his papers all over the floor. He would have seen me swinging the golf club but had chosen to say nothing and I certainly wasn't going to fill in the blanks, far less attempt to engage him in a conversation about stalking.

Golfing across Scotland is not something you readily confess to. I was conscious I might come across as the kind of chump who thinks it's outrageously anarchic to run a marathon dressed up as a vegetable, or to have a comedy sketch played at his funeral.

The path became thin and boggy and I was forced to play the ball short. I really needed to get three or four shots out of every Top Flite before I could afford to lose it.

I was now alongside the Allt a' Chaoil-reidhe, a broad, excitable burn. The walk-in had been strangely silent. Black, brooding lochs don't have much to say for themselves. Burns, however, make for manic company. The Allt a' Chaoil-reidhe chuckled away to itself. The sound of Scotland's mountains *is* that of water, pouring from hillsides, spewing over rocks, gurgling among the heather, an exuberant discourse that keeps you entertained for mile after mile.

Five stalking ponies lazed by the water, some of them munching grass, one sun-bathing on its side, all of them enjoying a period of rest. A swaying ladder-bridge carried me across the burn and the 254th shot rolled to a halt outside Culra Lodge bothy.

This building is maintained by the Mountain Bothies Association and is more habitable than most. There are single and double air-conditioned rooms and also a gym, two squash courts, a sauna, a bar and restaurant, and a swimming pool carved in the shape of Loch Ericht . . . Only kidding. It's no plusher than a steading. It does have a fireplace and it keeps the wind out, and that's about as good as it gets for a bothy. There was no basket of fruit or bouquet waiting, but I did find candles, a couple of soft seats, three single socks and two paperbacks, including *Vixen 03*, apparently a: 'towering new international superthriller'.

Over a bar of chocolate I read the more modest 'bothy book'. It was a new jotter, the old one having been destroyed a few months earlier in an act of vandalism at once both pathetic and monstrous. The book carried descriptions of where people had come from, where they were going, notes about the weather – the usual. Ian and Billy had become the 'talk of the place' after consuming 42 cans of Miller lager and a half-bottle of J.D. whisky in two days. One entry from a Russian visitor read: 'I think back home I'll tell friend mostly about these two days and night spended in the mountains more than about the days I spent in cities and towns of GB.'

The most recent visitors were Steve and Jez who had cycled in, but were repelled from Ben Alder by bad weather.

The Mountain Bothies Association was formed in 1965 and looks after around 100 shelters in the UK. The charity's aim is 'to maintain simple shelters in remote country for the use and benefit of all who love wild and lonely places'. The bothies belong to the landowners and the MBA asks walkers to respect their interests and 'show consideration for those who earn their living from the land'. Long stays and big groups are discouraged.

The MBA also feels compelled to point out that 'bothies are used entirely at your own risk' . . . Why? Are they worried someone will sue them if they nick their flesh on a nail or wake up to find a rat in their sleeping bag? How long before land-owners start ring-fencing estates with similar disclaimers about mountains?

> KEEP AWAY FROM CLIFFS
> THIN AIR IS DANGEROUS
> DO NOT ATTEMPT TO WALK ON IT

(How long before someone sues their parents for giving birth to them on the grounds they are doomed to die?)

People should be enormously grateful for organisations like the MBA. They shouldn't look for someone to blame if a bothy is a bit rough around the edges. In a blizzard a bothy is heaven. Culra might have lacked an en suite bathroom but it did provide the next best thing – a spade. Some wag had pinned instructions for its use on the wall:

> If you need to do a shite
> Don't piss around, do it right
> Take the spade, it's provided
> Dig a hole, cheeks divided
> Once you're done and wiped your arse
> Fill the hole, replace the grass
> Then walk off, you've done your bit
> At least you're not a lazy git

There was another sign outside the bothy, posted by a Deer Management Group which oversaw the three estates spanning Dalwhinnie and Kinlochleven – Ben Alder, Corrour and British Alcan. It said they recognised 'the tradition of free access to the hills' and welcomed walkers. However, it also stressed the importance of stalking in maintaining the health of both the red deer herd and the local economy, and asked for co-operation in this respect (i.e. keep to the paths during autumn). The tone was beseeching, almost apologetic.

With three holes to go and over eight hundred shots in hand, I was

# IN A RUT

confident of making or bettering 10,000. But within a few hundred yards of leaving the bothy my complacency ended. The path narrowed further and became stony. Thick heather lay to the right; the burn to the left. It was football terrain but I was reluctant to unleash the wobbling, orange orb with stalking taking place on the surrounding slopes. Deer have an acute sense of hearing and sight; I might have spooked a stag as a client squeezed the trigger.

And so I had to use one of two of my tennis balls. It was hard to hit cleanly and difficult to find afterwards. My pace also reduced. You focus on where a ball lands at the risk of stumbling on the rocks underfoot. Look down, then up, and the clump of heather you're using as a marker can easily blend with the next. But that's what I had to do to avoid twisting an ankle. Within quarter of a mile I lost a tennis ball.

So I decided to chance the football. The path was now hidden by some hillocks, but I couldn't risk hitting the football any further than the tennis ball. It took me more than 100 strokes to cover the first mile after Culra bothy.

The slopes of Ben Alder and Aonach Beag reared up as I pushed towards a pass that reaches nearly 2,500 feet. A waterfall crashes down the side of Ben Alder here, skidding between a gap in the cliff face. Across the sunless glen a herd of deer could be seen grazing at its foot. A few lifted their heads and looked towards me. There was no sign of a keeper or client but they would no doubt be prostrate among the heather, shambling across the ground like a couple of lizards, trying to get within 100 yards of the target. The keeper selects the stag and likes to see it killed with a single shot, usually to the chest.

As I drew level with the waterfall I put the football away.

Over the very next rise I found another keeper lying back in heather by the path, watching the herd with binoculars. He wore baggy tweeds and carried a walkie-talkie. A pony stood beside him, ready to carry the stag off the hill. Just as tweeds make ideal clothing for crawling through heather – tough, durable, warm when wet – the use of a pony is entirely pragmatic, not some Victorian affectation to please the shooters. The ground, this keeper told me, was too steep for an all-terrain vehicle.

'Besides, they make an awful mess.'

Throughout the year keepers kill many more hinds than clients shoot stags. They are asked to control Scotland's burgeoning red deer population with a singe-action rifle, a weapon that went out of fashion during the Boer War. When it comes to culling deer, a bazooka would be much more effective. Using an anti-tank device might not seem very sporting to the paying customer, but only because success is measured in terms of a singularly handsome kill. If the emphasis switched to the *number* of deer killed on a given day, the incentive would be there to go out and cause carnage.

'I don't think they'll ban deer-stalking,' said the keeper when I asked him about recent moves to outlaw bloodsports. 'They'll always need keepers.'

He worked on a neighbouring estate, had done the job for 16 years and described it as 'a good life'. When I mentioned the Mar estate he asked if I knew Willie Forbes.

'We send him about four heads a year,' he said.

As for the football, he suggested putting it away.

Fortunately the path straightened and I could again use golf balls, alternating with the last tennis ball.

The flanks of Ben Alder and Aonach Beag started to converge. Two golden eagles patrolled the sky above, one over each mountain, slicing back and forth like sentries, borne effortlessly by the warm air rising from the glen. Some walkers confuse the buzzard with the much bigger eagle. There are various ways to tell them apart at a distance (a buzzard for instance mews, while an eagle barks) but you should look at the background, not the bird. Only an eagle could thrive among these gigantic bald hills, without road-kill or a glut of rabbits to subsist on.

Just over 500 shots brought me to the bealach. The keeper had described this as the 'dark' glen but I found it perfectly relaxing – despite its being surrounded by fragments of helicopter wreckage.

Ben Alder is, however, a place of torment and death. In 1996 a man's badly decomposed body was found on the mountain's western slope, having lain there for six months. His wallet had been emptied and the labels cut from his clothing. He had been shot in the chest, a revolver was next to his body. Forensic anthropologists reconstructed his face and 18 months later 26 year old Frenchman Emmanuel Caillet was identified after Interpol circulated the image. Police were confident the man had committed suicide but his distraught father suggested he had been murdered in a role-playing game that had gone too far.

On 30 December 1951, a party of five walkers from the Glasgow-based Glencoe Mountaineering Club perished in a storm at the top of this pass. They had planned to spend New Year in the wilds. All were in their twenties, including the newly married Anne Tewnion, the youngest at 22, and the only survivor. Somehow, she made it down to the lodge at the head of Loch Ossian, four miles away. Her husband Sidney was among the dead.

Joss Gosling, then a member of the RAF Kinloss Mountain Rescue, explained in a letter:

> Many of the estate workers had already done the ground work in finding the bodies, helped by folk at the Youth Hostel, so when we arrived we had to escort the bodies to Corrour Station and take them to Fort William by train. Two of the party are buried in the graveyard at Glen Nevis with the names of the other two on the headstone. As to walking alone in the hills, there will always be misfortune but I myself enjoyed many days on the hill solo because of no one I knew having the same interest. I'm in my seventies now, luckily living in Fort William with people who seem to enjoy walking with me so I can always find company and I can assure you that mountain rescuers understand, providing that people equip themselves well and to the best of their ability use commonsense. Back to Corrour, remember that outdoor clothing and equipment in those days was not the best.

If you walk alone you increase your risk but also your pleasure. I was throrougly enjoying the break from my own voice. Professor Hugh Pennington's views are also worth noting:

> Some sociologists claim that we now live in a 'risk society' — there is an obsession everywhere with doom just around the corner and an overwhelming desire to seek safety wherever we can. So the notion that we should worry about hazards in the countryside, rather than accept them as a part of the buffetings of ordinary life as our grandparents did, is easy to explain. It cannot be denied that people fall off mountains and meet sticky ends by driving too fast on rural roads. But having said that it has to be admitted that the overwhelming majority of people who live in and visit the countryside survive to tell the tale, and so as a generalisation it is pretty safe. Being infected by E.coli 0157 joins falling off Lochnagar or being struck by lightning on a golf course as real rural hazards. They all happen. But not often — and there are simple ways to make them rarer!

Also, a bothy to the south of Ben Alder is supposed to be haunted by the ghost of an estate worker who hanged himself from the rafters.

All in all, then, the makings of a macabre tour. The most famous mountain spook, though, is probably the 'Big Grey Man' of Ben Macdui. This towering apparition sent Victorian mountaineer Professor Norman Collie running from the top and his experience did much to promote the existence of things supernatural in Scotland's mountains. In subsequent years walkers and spiritualists alike flocked to Ben Macdui. So, it seems, did hundreds of obliging Grey Men.

Loch Ossian lies at the bottom of a glen, framed by dark pines. I followed the path along the flank of Ben Alder for a mile before dropping towards a burn that runs into it.

For the first time this trip I heard a stag roaring – a cross between the cry of a humpback whale and a particularly pugnacious sheep. The stag and his harem clung to the southern slopes of Aonach Beag; another eagle circled thousands of feet above them. I'd been told stalking was also taking place in this glen, so I couldn't use the football while the deer were within sight. One yawning peat bog followed another. In crossing this melting black desert I had no option but to incur a fifty stroke penalty, my seventh of the round.

Within quarter of a mile a path had appeared alongside a burn born only a mile away but already tumbling over itself with youthful energy. There were patches of flat, open grass suitable for a Top Flite, but for most of the descent I struggled with the football. Occasionally it would end up in the burn where it would lilt along for few dozen yards, accelerate between some big boulders, then wedge fast. Under Rule 26-2, I could play the ball from within the water hazard. So I let it coast and just spooned it back on the bank with the club.

Strath Ossian opened out northwards. My eye was drawn to a vehicle track running across its western side like a zip. At its end, mountains appeared darkly swollen in the fading afternoon light: a collection of bruises on the horizon. Throughout the day clouds had boarded up the blue sky, multiplying with the gusto of a virus. Only the perverse could romanticise this cadaverous landscape. At that moment I liked Scotland rather less.

As I reached the first pine trees an all-terrain vehicle surged past, bucking wildly as it went. A man in a commando jacket was at the controls and a stag was in the back, its body quivering with the jolts from the bumpy path.

When I worked on the Mar estate we brought a stag in on a pony. The deer was emptied of its stomach and intestines on the hillside ('gralloched') before being strapped tightly to the pony's back. The head was tied across the saddle where the antlers wouldn't puncture the pony's flanks had it slipped in the heather.

The 'guests' did little more than pull the trigger, though some barely managed this after dragging their own bodies through the heather. The whole business reminded me of a child sitting on its father's knee and being allowed to 'drive' the family car. Those killing a stag for the first time would daub their shiny, already red cheeks with blood. Some, apparently, ended up on the pony which carried them back to the Land-rover, leaving the ghillie to drag the stag by the antlers.

They rarely missed their target, but then the keeper brought them to within stoning distance of the deer. An injured stag runs and hides, and if disturbed runs until it drops. It is imperative, then, that the second bullet brings it down.

The keeper I worked with once described watching an injured animal halt half a mile away. He pointed the guest's gun at the deer, raising it slightly to allow for the parabolic flight of the bullet, the gun's accuracy woefully distorted by gravity. The stag keeled over on the spot. The keeper was amazed, but not as much as the man to whom he calmly handed the rifle back.

He let people shoot only old and sick animals, never a handsome stag in its prime. He could tell if animal had liver-flukes simply by studying its eyes . . . from 50 yards away. One guest chose to kill a different, prettier stag and was marched back to his car. He complained to the laird who stood by the keeper. Another guest lost his gold watch on the hill. The wily keeper was able to retrace their steps across the heather and find it.

It's the pungency of the blood I remember most from this time – the smell of a butcher's shop without the mask of sawdust. Much of the blood was drained when the animal was gralloched but the back of the Land-rover still needed swilling-out every evening. I was struck by the fact a deer was at least as heavy as a man. For their efforts in squashing this oversized fly, the ghillies were given the liver to eat, so we might savour both the taste and the ritual.

I never saw a stag being shot; I always waited with the pony. My friend, Gordon McPherson, spent two seasons on Mar rather than the few weeks I did, and was invited to shoot a stag towards the end of the year. He hit the head rather than the chest and the keeper finished the animal off by thrusting a knife into its heart.

Ben Alder estate and Corrour estate, which I had now reached, are working together to offer top-quality stalking. A new three million pound lodge is being completed on the shore of Loch Ossian after the last one burned to the ground in the 1940s. The five-storey, eight-bedroom building will be let to shooting and stalking parties for around twenty-five thousand pounds a week.

It was designed by internationally renowned architect, Moshe Safdie, who wanted to 'echo and express the essence of Highland architecture' and to create 'an authentic expression of the spirit of today'. The Royal Fine Art Commission of Scotland supported the planning application, tipping the lodge to become one of the 'few examples of world-class late twentieth-century architecture in Scotland'. Six Lochaber councillors were left to say 'yes' or 'no' to the lodge. The vote was carried by four to two.

Builders continued to work as the daylight started to ebb. The headstrong burn had merged with the River Ossian, which flowed unhurried between the trees, dark and treacly. The terrain around the hunting lodge is flat, green and rural. Golf ball terrain. I pitched along the vehicle track. A few people walked by but said nothing.

On the south side of the loch I reverted to the tennis ball. The track was stony and bounded by rhododendrons and drainage ditches overflowing with lush, golf ball-swallowing moss. These last few miles were a genuine effort. Each step hurt; it felt like I'd staved both thighs. I nudged the ball forwards, past slanting rowan trees and the inky loch, until finally I reached the youth hostel where two tame stags grazed outside. One scratched its cheek with its hind foot.

They reminded me of a grizzled old stag that used to hang around the Mar estate. The animal would sometimes wander among the vehicles as we prepared to set off in the morning, but the keeper never had the heart to shoot it. He could always find it on the hill, and would lead excited guests close to this magnificent animal, which had a full set of antlers. It would have happily let you pat it but they weren't to know that. The stag was thought to be senile. That, or a very clever fake.

**STROKES: 1134    TOTAL: 8083    SCORE: -949**

## *Playing Solo*

The Rules of Golf treat the solo player as a second-class citizen: 'Two-ball matches should have precedence and be entitled to pass any three- or four-ball match, which should invite them through. A single player has no standing and should give way to a match of any kind.' That is a mistake. Golf is not a game fought between other men and women, but between you and the course. A golfer will happily finish last if he improves his personal best. If you were the last person left on earth, you could still lose yourself in a round of golf. Sinking a long putt would bring pleasure and missing a short one consternation. Solo golf teaches you patience and honesty. When you tee-off on a summer dawn, and are the first to trespass the dew-covered greens, there's nobody to kid but yourself.

## SEVENTEEN

# Trainspotting

| HOLE 17 | DISTANCE: 15 MILES | PAR: 937 |
| --- | --- | --- |

WHILE I ENJOY the anonymity of a big hotel (being a room number, part of the honeycomb) the indulgence of a stay always leaves me feeling slightly uncomfortable – all those hot baths, all those uneaten pillow mints. The bed appears to make itself when you're out, clothes fold themselves over chairs, the fridge refills with beer, shit vanishes from the toilet bowl. A hotel leaves you perfumed, pasteurised, not quite human. It's like being back in the womb.

A Youth Hostel offers a rawer experience. It does nothing to deny your existence as an out-sized baby.

Every hostel seems to carry a whiff of stale sweat – a trademark smell that seems to be made to a recipe. It's an honest odour, however, unlike the chemical sprays used to fumigate hotels. When you arrive in a hostel, there is usually someone in the kitchen making a meal from scratch, chopping and boiling vegetables, letting the aroma of the juices mix with your own.

You hear people chew, snore, belch and fart like cows in a field. Their tooth-brushing sounds unexpectedly vigorous, almost violent. Even another's shaving can be noisy. And should you be in any doubt about how much keeping we humans take, there's still a chance you will be given a domestic chore to do. Can you imagine being asked to clean the toilets before checking out of a Holiday Inn? ('*Just those on the third floor, sir . . .*' )

'I prefer people to do things themselves,' said Thomas, who with his wife was looking after the Loch Ossian hostel. 'I don't like to tell them "you do this, you do that".' Looking around at the orderly, scrubbed kitchen, I told him I was open to suggestions. 'There's nothing to do,' he said. 'We're light on numbers.'

Thomas, from Germany, took charge nearly two years ago. The Loch Ossian hostel closes over winter, although groups may rent it then. Thomas spends the dark months reading. 'When you work for seven months a year without a day off, you deserve to semi-hibernate,' he said. He wouldn't have been much more than 30. 'We don't make plans,' he said. 'If we like it, we'll stay on.'

'Youth Hostel' is a misnomer these days. You're as likely to find yourself sharing living space with a pensioner. A small, grey, zestful woman was pacing the kitchen when I arrived. Lillian had spent the day walking round Loch Ossian and was waiting for friends to join her for an annual get-together. Two of them arrived shortly after me, collapsing through the door after hiking twenty miles from Fort William.

I hadn't stayed in a youth hostel for years and it was a shock to be reminded that men and women sleep in separate quarters. At Loch Ossian the two dormitories abut a room housing the kitchen and canteen. The water used for cooking and washing is drawn directly from the loch. A propeller on a pole normally generates what electricity is needed, but the recent days had been windless and we were forced to cook using gas.

Talk turned to food – its production, the crazy subsidy system, supermarkets' reluctance to stock British produce, the cooking of food, the eating of it. Slumped on a bench, sipping weak tea, I said less and less. By 8 p.m. I was close to nodding off. The conversation took on a dreamy, disjointed air.

'But the preserved ginger in a pot – I put that in rhubarb.'

'We've got ginger marmalade.'

'Yes, we've got ginger marmalade. I don't seem to be eating a lot of jam these days.'

'The more ginger, the better. Now Frances, like me, loves ginger.'

I went to bed, leaving my fellow hostellers discussing the pros and cons of teabag draw-strings.

Breakfast was the same as supper: a curry-flavoured Pot Noodle and a sachet of chocolate-flavoured Complan, the 'complete meal in a drink' favoured by 'athletes and convalescents'. I had just 68 golf balls left. If I'd been smart I'd have posted another hundred or so to the hostel. I did try to send some to Corrour Station, a mile away, but Red Star refused to make a drop, military style, on the unstaffed platform.

It was dull but dry. Within seven shots of leaving the hostel I ran into Max, a playful collie, who snaffled the tennis ball. 'Are you playing golf or tennis?' his owner asked sarcastically, handing the ball back.

I reached Corrour Station in exactly 60 shots. A dozen people were stepping off a train – three of them with mountain bikes, the rest in gaitors and Gore-tex.

The former signal box is now a bunkhouse. There's also a licensed restaurant where you can dine by candlelight. It is modelled on a Victorian station, painted dark green and white, with red bricks at one end and a big clock with Roman numerals above the entrance. Corrour Station is the sort of place Hercule Poirot might disembark at and implicate you in some heinous crime, possibly involving the death of an international industrialist, a stalking party and set of bloodied antlers.

I left my rucksack and club at the door, slipped off my waistcoat, and went in. A Pot Noodle and a Complan drink may pack enough calories to get you through the day, but they don't taste anything like as good as a fried egg roll.

'Are you walking or running?' asked Rick Brown as he took my order.

'Golfing.'

# PAR 10,000

Before taking over Corrour Station House, Rick spent 22 years in the army. The job took him around Europe, where he climbed mountains and taught colleagues to ski. Here, on this high, empty moor, he has at last put down roots, anchored by a railway that connects Scotland's modern heart with its mythical one. The track isn't there to amuse tourists. Eight trains pass through here every day, rebounding between the Central Belt and the Highlands, crossing Rannoch Moor and hugging the plunging side of Loch Treig as they go.

Rick and his wife Angela run the restaurant like a franchise. It was built by Lisbet and Josef Koerner who paid £3.4 million for Corrour estate in 1995. Both are professors at Harvard University; she is a member of the Rausing family, which made its multi-billion-pound fortune from a packaging patent for drinks' cartons. Far from discouraging walkers, they appear to want to make them feel at home. On one side of the track there's the promise of a proper meal, on the other 14 waiting beds.

Corrour's changing ownership is described in *A History of a Sporting Estate*, written by Lisbet Koerner and David Dick.

In 1834 the Duke of Gordon sold the estate to a Dumfriesshire family, the Walkers of Crawfordtown, who had made their money trading goods from the West Indies. They were determined to make Corrour pay for itself, and catered for Victorian grouse-shooters who would arrive by train, ride in a horse and carriage to the western end of Loch Ossian, and from there board a steamboat to the lodge. Although the estate made as much as £3,500 from shooting in 1911, grouse numbers fluctuated wildly. Some years were much less bountiful and deer stalking came to be seen as more of a dependable source of income.

The Walkers sold Corrour to Sir John Stirling Maxwell of Glasgow in 1891. Making money wasn't his main aim. He planted trees, improved the housing for estate workers (with baths and indoor toilets no less) and helped find the community a qualified teacher. He even provided land for the Youth Hostel so walkers would have somewhere to stay. Following the hard post-war years his family sold Corrour to the Forestry Commission but they shrewdly retained the sporting rights, and bought it back in the 1980s.

Since then the proliferation of people on the hill has driven deer into more remote corries where the grazing is poorer. In a poor environment, body size reduces and the condition of successive generations has deteriorated as a result. An industry supporting 350 full-time jobs is being put at risk. Knowing this, and having heard stalkers describe the shortage of 'really big' stags, I was left wondering if the time hasn't come to start culling hillwalkers.

Rick said I'd have to sprint to make Kinlochleven by dark. A boggy path runs alongside the railway, straddled in places with sleepers. Within half a mile I peeled left towards the northern spur of Leum Uilleim, switching from golf ball to football and back again as I climbed above the man-eating peat bogs, and followed a faint vehicle-track to the cloud base at 2,000 feet.

It was here that Tommy tried to drag his mates out walking in the film *Trainspotting*. Confronted with this desolate scene, Spud immediately observed it 'wasn't natural'. When Tommy asked if it didn't make them proud to be Scottish, Renton scorned: 'It's shite being Scottish . . . We're the most wretched, miserable, servile, pathetic trash that was ever shat into existence.'

His rejoinder got the biggest laugh in the film, the most ringing endorsement. Indeed, so traumatised were Renton and his mates that they made 'a healthy, informed, democratic decision to get back on heroin as soon as possible'.

Leum Uilleim, it must be said, is an unremarkable hill. If An Tellach is a compound fracture of the land – splintered rock bursting through the skin – Leum Uilleim is a mild contusion. You expect it to deflate under your feet, to spread-out beneath you and form a new heather moor. It's the kind of hill that gives Scotland a bad name, that betrays our snowy-peaked tea-towels and other fanciful Highland souvenirs.

With a golf club in my hand though, it became one of the most interesting I have climbed.

I worked out I could afford to take 120 strokes a mile from here and I'd still break 10,000. That meant nudging the ball 40 feet with each stroke – easy enough. But the equipment could still let me down. If the football was gored by a stag or burst in some other way, I'd have to use the tennis ball which couldn't be hit in deep heather more than a few feet. I cursed not packing a beach ball for emergencies.

On the northern side of the spur I used the football for the long slide towards Gleann Iolairean. The path that runs through the glen is too rough and sinuous for proper golf. Even with the football I had to move above or below it to strike the ball. I managed to fire-off a Top Flite every 20 shots or so, and this helped keep the score down.

In a field you will always find a decent lie and have a chance of recovering the ball, providing you don't hit it too far. In the hills my average score was turning out to be much the same but my play was considerably more erratic and the ball-loss far higher. It was fortunate I had managed to source hundreds of cheap balls before reaching the heather.

Anyway, back to the 17th and your commentator.

> Thank you. Well, Ewen's ball is sitting up quite nicely in the heather. He has a shot of some 15 yards to the path. There's still very little wind to work with but the ground breaks sharply from right to left and I fancy he might use that to his advantage . . . He can't see the flag from where he is but I'll mark it on your screen . . . there . . . nearly ten miles away. There's a small mountain to cross and a tricky water hazard in the shape of Loch Eilde Mor, but if he can get down in 1,000 from here he should be okay.

The path continued to trickle down through the glen and the burn opened out just below it. A sward appeared like some heavenly green amid the stones and marsh and heather. Judging from the tattered, rusting fence around it, this was former grazing ground. But within a few shots the soft, short grass was behind me, gone like a mirage. Finally I reached Loch Chiarain. I took care not to hook the football into the still water. There was no wind or current to usher it back and I didn't want to go in after it.

> Golfer drowns trying to save ball.
> 'Bloody fool,' says Mountain Rescue.

After 569 shots I arrived at Loch Chiarain bothy, which is set back from the water with a couple of acres of grass out front. Perfect for pitch and putt, I thought.

This was another MBA bothy: clean and tidy and unlikely to fall down on your head. No trouser-press, of course, but there was a brush and a spade and a wheelbarrow for mixing cement should you have felt like a spot of pointing in the middle of the night. A plastic chair had been placed in the centre of the bare attic floor, looking rather sinister. I assumed this was where members of the MBA elite had swooped to interrogate a hillwalker who failed to respect the bothy code.

('*We know it's in here somewhere . . . Tell us where you hid the shit!*')

I continued towards Blackwater Reservoir. Three thousand men took eight years to build this dam, which could pass for the work of a glacier.

In contrast, the surrounding grey-brown hills look as though they have been teased into shape by the wind, like leaves in a park. Towards the west, clouds had snagged and burst on the bigger mountains, spilling their contents over an area that gets six feet of rain a year. I veered away from Blackwater Reservoir towards the wetness, alone in this sombre, twilit land. . . .

Glen Coe – the gloomiest glen of all – lies a few miles to the south of here. Being the site of a massacre doesn't make for a party atmosphere. In 1692, 120 men from Clan Campbell fell upon the rebel MacDonalds, supporters of the newly deposed Catholic King, James II, and put 38 men and boys to their deaths.

The Campbells, purporting to march north, were guests of the MacDonalds, who were obliged to furnish the Government's soldiers with food and shelter. Even in the seventeenth century, killing your host was considered a major social gaffe. Tradition required that you *defend* him while digesting your most recent meal and such 'murder under trust' excited as much public horror as the brutality of the massacre itself. The killing might have been less abhorrent had the Campbells foregone supper that evening, done the deed, *then* sat down to eat. Some historians believe the Campbells were fully aware of the faux pas they were about to commit and didn't want to slay the MacDonalds. Legend records one Campbell soldier pausing in the glen and saying, 'If you knew what was to happen here tonight, great stone, you would be up and away' – but then why whisper it to a stone?

As I pressed on, the golf helped lighten the mood. I could now land a Top Flite within ten feet of the path – enough to find it three or four times before losing it altogether. My game had been turned on its head. PGA coach Hamish Love had fettled the swing; over 100 miles of field, road, moor and mountain had formed the practice area. Some golfers boast they have never had a lesson. They want us to admire their nebulous potential, not their indifferent play. One of the joys of getting older is an almost gleeful acceptance of your short-comings. It's a relief to admit you're no damned good at something, that you need some help.

I used to swing a driver like I was trying to kill the ball. (The guys in *Casino* with the baseball bats who pulverize Joe Pesci – *they* had more finesse.) But over the summer, thought had replaced thuggery. My right foot was now fixed to the ground and the left did the flouncing. My hands overlapped, the right having been cranked through a quarter turn. The club face ended up pointing at the earth and not the sky. Few golfers display Tiger Woods's athletic flair, but fewer still his assiduous, analytical intelligence. To have done nothing more than hit one ball after another would have made me a very good bad golfer.

The rain had thickened. There was barely any wind, which made it cloying. The drops beaded on my clothes like sweat. I opted to leave the last few Top Flites in my pocket in the hope there would be a broad path ahead where I would get maybe ten shots out of a ball before losing it. Even with the football it was arduous going. I was climbing towards the 2,000-foot southern spur of Glas Bheinn over increasingly soggy-yet-rocky ground. Just short of the cloud-covered ridge, I picked the ball up. The conditions had become marginal for golf. I would accept a 50-stroke penalty and keep my resolve intact for the other side.

At the top I sat down next to a cross made from sticks and choked back the last chunks of my *Fruit and Nut*. I reckon this cross marked the top, nothing more. You can scatter ashes in the mountains but not bodies. Rick Brown had shown me a photograph of the four dead walkers being taken off that hill in December 1951 – Corrour Station under snow, men in bonnets by a train, the bodies somewhere behind them.

Glas Bheinn was just as rough on the other side but the football had gravity on its side and bounded ahead. Loch Eilde Mor opened out through the murk, a sliver of water between cloud-flattened hills. The muddy path kept high on the bank and I could be brazen with the football, swerving it across the heather. Across the loch, groups of walkers moved steadily in the other direction, presumably towards an overnight camp. They were the first people I had seen in nearly ten miles.

I joined a vehicle track and fired off the last few golf balls; there was no point in holding onto them any longer. I passed yet another implausible sign:

> BEWARE! FOOTPATH WORK IN PROGRESS
> ON BEHALF OF KINLOCHLEVEN LAND DEVELOPMENT.
> A TEAM OF OUR PROFESSIONAL PATH WORKERS ARE
> CARRYING OUT REPAIRS AND CONSTRUCTION
> WORK ON THIS SITE.
> PLEASE PROCEED WITH CAUTION.

This was directed at walkers coming the other way. Anybody approaching from the west, as I had done, was likely to stumble upon

. . . well, what exactly? Somebody mixing cement? Or tapping a stone into place with a trowel? ('*Look out, he's got a spirit level!*')

As I descended the last hill in the mist, half a dozen sheep scattered in the path of the ball. I'd seen very few these last 40 miles. The hill-farming support scheme is due to be scrapped within a couple of years, when, under the Europe's agricultural policy, subsidy will no longer be paid on the number of animals farmed but on the acreage. Small tenant crofters fear they will go bankrupt. Landowners are expected to replace sheep with birch trees, the planting of which attracts handsome grants.

So there you have it. We got rid of the trees to make way for people, then got rid of the people to make way for sheep. Now we're going to get rid of the sheep to make way for trees. Humans are clearly interlopers in all of this.

Kinlochleven spread out below the thinning cloud with the pleasing precision of a model railway set. Its white houses are neatly ordered like those in any town built around a single service or industry, in this case an aluminium smelter.

The last quarter-mile was the steepest ground I had encountered in the whole trip; too steep to play in the opposite direction. A tap with the club sent the football charging off down the hillside, like an unleashed dog dashing home. After 200 yards the slope eased off but I couldn't find the ball. As I searched among the ferns I became aware of two gorges falling on either side. The ball had almost certainly slipped over. My faithful companion was gone . . .

This just left the tennis ball, which I managed to shepherd to the foot of the slope, checking any escape bid with the club. I caught a couple walking ahead. Rather than letting them get in front to clear a path for the ball, I trundled it along behind them, making cursory putts of no more than ten feet. Wet, sore, tired and hungry, I emerged onto the pavement beside St Paul's church, half a mile short of the finish.

**STROKES: 1316    TOTAL: 9399    SCORE: -570**

# The Perfect Round

Whenever you step onto the first tee, even when you are old and shrunken and the club feels heavy in your hands, this will always be the start of The Perfect Round. Whether you are playing as part of a team or ostensibly to have fun, you will be flirting with your own score, noting its intentions at least as far as the second shot, or maybe the second hole – or wherever it falls apart. However, the difference between a professional player and an amateur is almost beyond imagining. Let's say you normally par 17 out of the 18 holes on a golf course. What, then, is the probability of you playing like a pro – that is, failing to drop any strokes? Around three to one. If you normally par half the holes, your odds of having a scratch round explode to quarter of a million to one. And if you usually make only one par in a round, you're a forty-thousand-million-billion-to-one shot to play to par.

## EIGHTEEN

# The Putt that Never Drops

| HOLE 18 | DISTANCE: 0.5 MILES | PAR: 31 |
| --- | --- | --- |

WHEN IT CAME to hitting the last shot, I had decided to treat myself to a decent ball – a brand new Callaway Rule 35.

# THE PERFECT ROUND

'With all the graphs, statistics and techno-speak out there, buying golf balls has become the most complicated part of golf,' said the sales brochure. Personally, I've never struggled with this aspect of the game. You just go into a pro-shop, announce 'I'll have a pack of these' and hand over some cash. Holing out from 40 feet on a links green, figuring the angles on the runs and borrows, gauging the coefficient of friction – that might call for an 800 MHz brain. Of course Callaway can't resist indulging in some techno-speak of its own:

> With optimised aerodynamics and the thinnest cover of any ball of its kind, Rule 35's distance off the tee is amazing... A precise combination of the incredibly large core, the ultra-thin boundary layer and the soft cover offers both spin and control . . . We laser-measure and X-ray every single Rule 35 golf ball . . .

Some hospitals in Britain would kill for that kind of technology. It's no surprise the Callaway factory cost $170 million.

'So there's only one question left,' said the brochure. 'Do you prefer Softfeel or Firmfeel?'

I'm afraid that kind of subtlety is lost on someone who is happy golfing with a big, orange football. I went for the one with the blue logo.

A single shot would send this virgin ball to the bottom of Loch Leven. Its outstanding durability (made possible by a 'unique blend of materials proprietary to Callaway Golf') would go untested. It would lie among the silt and pebbles, accruing slime and weed, its pristine skin yellowing over the years, until it too looked like a mottled fragment of the earth's crust. And there it would remain, bobbling across the loch bed, stroked back and forth by tidal currents, one shot shaping the next. The putt that never drops.

But first the ball needed to be blessed.

The Rev. Canon David Day admitted that 20 years ago he would never have entertained such a request, one that might have sounded flippant or exploitative. But, two years away from retirement, he was a changed man.

'I've grown to see God in a wider way,' he explained. 'He is a God of surprises. You never know where you're going to encounter him. I've come to know his presence, but not in a "holy, holy" way.' Canon Day (an itinerant West Highland priest whose churches include St Paul's here) said he wasn't planning 'to make the sign of a cross over a golf ball' – a meaningless gesture. Instead, he was prepared to accept the Callaway and what it represented as an offering within the context of the service.

We met beforehand in his Duror home to discuss the service and what significance it might have for a lapsed Protestant.

I explained I had belonged to a scripture union group at school, but had become disillusioned with religion when I discovered all non-practising Christians were bound for hell. The doomed included my mum and dad. They weren't diabolists or anything, but neither had they professed any great love for Jesus. I desperately wanted to tip them off about hell but was too shy to, and took to shadowing them everywhere they went, ready to reveal all if they looked like dying on me.

If hell wasn't off-putting enough, many of those who attended the group came across like the kids in *The Village of the Damned*. Children should be full of questions: they were full of answers. I was left to conclude that if God created Man, conceit created God.

Canon Day and I spent an hour going through the service so that I might present the golf ball with some sincerity.

'Christianity is too obsessed with sin,' he said. 'We shouldn't say to people "do you know how big a sinner you are, but do you know how much God loves you?" The world isn't full of sin. It's just broken.'

His reading of the Bible was less prescriptive than my scripture union leader's. This allowed us both to approach the idea of the blessing obliquely. All I had done was knock a golf ball across some hills. I hadn't undergone any kind of epiphany and wasn't about to join the Episcopal Church. But I had learned to look at my surroundings from different perspectives, to read the runs and borrows of history, even to conceive of some divine order, and Canon Day thought this was something worth sharing.

Sunday morning was cool and fresh, the grass mint-green with dew. The heavy rain had passed, washing away any vestige of summer. Bracken lay rusting and collapsing on the hillsides. Trees had turned rigid with the shock of autumn; their papery leaves sashayed to the ground like snowflakes. Berries had started to shrivel. No amount of rain would revive this desiccated land. The earth had already started to shrink at the touch of the coming winter.

I had spent the night in a hired caravan, drinking bramble whisky liqueur with two friends, Roy and Louise. They had driven to Fort William to climb Ben Nevis but changed their minds when they saw the rain. As I tumbled off the hillside at St Paul's, they'd rolled up in their car, having already tried the pub. The only dry clothes I had were waterproof trousers (not the nicest material to wear next to your skin) so it was a relief to find Roy had a spare pair of jogger bottoms. He also gave me his walking boots. Several sizes too big, they left me flopping around like a clown – a sad-faced clown whose steam-cooked blisters were starting to rise.

Just after 9 a.m. we arrived at St Paul's. It was a refreshingly simple place of worship, modest in its dimensions and without pretension in its architecture. The original wooden structure was erected in 1908 when the smelter opened and was being rebuilt in the 1950s along with the village houses.

Canon Day was there to greet us in a long, white tunic. We joined the small congregation, sang some bouncy hymns, and listened to Canon Day, who described faith as 'stepping out into a world both wonderful and dangerous', and as 'losing oneself for the greater glory of God', rather than being an act of 'self-preservation'. The golf ball, wrapped in pink and peach paper tissues tied with a hair-band, became just another offering on the altar. It was placed beside the bread and the silver goblet that held the wine.

The congregation offered the bread and wine in remembrance of Jesus and what he did for the world. I expressed gratitude for being alive and having had the vitality to walk across the strip of land I call my country. Towards the end of the service Canon Day beckoned me forward and placed the ball in my palm.

'Bless you, David,' he said quietly.

After the service and a cup of coffee, Roy, Louise and I passed through the village.

An exibition called 'The Aluminium Story' was taking place. It began over 80 years ago and came to an end on 20 June 2000, when the smelter closed with the loss of 51 jobs. It was once the biggest in the world, employing nearly 1,000 people, and brought electiricty to the village before Glasgow and London had theirs. Ore was shipped in and huge amounts of power, generated by the Blackwater dam, turned it into aluminium. British Alcan's hydro-electric station will continue to operate and eventually feed into the national grid.

'They've no wages to pay, you see,' said one villager, referring to the reduction in overheads. He quickly checked his bitterness, though.

'The company has been very good to the village. If the community ever needed anything, they provided it.' Redundant staff received re-training in skills such as hotel management and digger driving. They may yet find jobs close to home; millions are being invested in new businesses in the Lochaber area. There's talk of building a brewery in place of the smelter, and an outdoor activities centre in Kinlochleven.

# PAR 10,000

I left the main road just beyond the exhibition. The final hole ran past a football pitch, between gorse bushes, and along the bank of the River Leven where jellyfish marked high tide. A woman stood on the other side of the river holding a cat in her arms.

'He's part wildcat,' she shouted across. 'He's a stray but very tame.' She called him Zebedee. 'From the bible,' she explained. It was then that I recognised her from the congregation at St Paul's.

I chipped the tennis ball towards the shore, taking care not to slice it into the river-channel. Eventually I stood on a jetty of grass – a tee almost – looking out over the black-brown loch. It carried the reflections of a lone fishing boat and the triangular peaks rising either side. A wisp of cloud curled around the Pap of Glencoe like a halo.

I picked up the tennis ball for one last time and replaced it with the Callaway.

Addressing the ball, I drew the five-iron steadily backwards, keeping my left foot flat on the ground, turning my shoulders more than my hips, loading the muscles around my torso, shifting weight to my right side. My hands were relaxed, my left arm straight; head down, bum out.

At the top of the swing a twinge of nervous excitement threatened to disturb my equilibrium – this was one shot I didn't want to squelch – but I hung in there, uncoiling my body no more hurriedly than I had wound it up. The iron fell upon the ball like a pendulum, retracing its path, guided by the latent energy.

Contact.

A tiny tremor ran up through the shaft, its frequency blending with the sound of the club smacking the ball, the discharge crisp and reassuring. It wasn't anything like perfect – I was still cocking my wrists too early, straightening my right leg, not closing the club face enough on the follow-through – but it was a quantum improvement on that first shot I played from Foveran links. The Callaway leapt into the smoky-blue sky, hung there for a moment, and dropped with a glutinous plop into a trench of water near the steep northern shore.

Nine thousand, four hundred and thirty-four . . .

As I started to walk back to the car, the ripples were still spreading across the loch.

I'll leave the last word to someone who understands golf better than I ever will. When the world turned its glare onto the teenage Tiger Woods, who had just spent that season routing the opposition, he recalled some advice given to him by his father:

You will never become bigger than any sport you play. That is the fact of reality. If you think you are, you have the wrong perspective. You are there to compete and play in the sport you enjoy and, more importantly, to enhance it. I have had a lovely summer.

Me too, Tiger, me too.

**STROKES: 35       TOTAL: 9434      SCORE: -566**

# *The Nineteenth Hole*

The nineteenth hole doesn't exist. It is a golfing joke, referring to the clubhouse where golfers go to ruminate on their rounds and drink beer. This is a hallowed place. Golfers must remove their spiked shoes before entering – although many would be steadier on their feet when leaving if they kept them on. The clubhouse usually affords a view of the first tee and the 18th green. As you start or finish your round, there is a sense all eyes are upon you, judging you, when most folk are actually staring at menus, trying to decide whether to have the scampi or the chicken for lunch. They are safe inside the clubhouse after all, warmed up or cooled down, spruce again – and ready to confirm the truism that most golfers hit their best shots when others aren't watching.

# NINETEEN

# Solitaire in a Field

FIVE HUNDRED and sixty-six under par is pretty good. That's 68 on the Old Course. This would indicate that I went from being a very average golfer to a world-beater in a matter of months – or that the par I set for crossing Scotland was far too high. As I'm confident I'd still take 95 shots to get round the St Andrews course, maybe this book should be called *Par 7,150.*

Scotland really is a slip of a country. At its narrowest point it is just 50 miles across. I took 18 days to traverse one of the broadest parts, averaging a languorous 9 miles a day. You can always find an easy way through our mountains because they are small and have few sharp edges, certainly compared to those on the Continent. The greatest geographical barriers were the Rivers Dee and Spey, both of which could have been swum across by anyone capable of completing a length of their local baths.

I had set out in search of boyhood thrills and had found a few: playing with a ball on the road; nipping into gardens to fetch it; hiding in bushes from cars; not wearing a jacket in the rain; not telling people where I was going; poking around derelict buildings; being chased by farmyard animals; tramping through puddles; climbing trees; falling into burns; dressing up as a soldier . . . being cheeky.

Back to that front lawn of mine. The ball I rashly hit towards a neighbour's house as a boy could just as easily have found the River Dee. The river was an abiding thrill for me then. It filled with snow in winter and darting black eels in summer. In spate it moved with a terrifying, silent, power. My pals and I would stand and watch whole trees cartwheeling towards the sea. I used to feel sorry for city kids. We had beech trunks to carve our names on; they only had walls to spray. (This was a ridiculous conceit of course. Today, kids just spray the trees.) Growing up in Peterculter, then, left the stink of the countryside on my soul which years of living in a vibrant city centre has done nothing to shift. Maybe I should get out into the garden more.

I can't pretend to have any affinity with the terse, phlegmatic men and women who work the soil, but I do admire the essential honesty of their labour and its indubitable worth. They could be forgiven for treating with disdain those of us who sit in front of a computer all day. I also have a sneaking regard for any farmer brassy enough to ride around in a Range-rover while claiming state support . . .

But beyond this, walking across Scotland gave me no great sense of belonging. The mountains and rivers surely didn't shape our character – they preserved its diversity. They kept people and their customs apart; they formed borders within borders; they give rise to Highlanders and Lowlanders and bitter division. There wasn't a huge amount of open trade among early clans, only guerrilla warfare.

When the opportunity for self-government arose, we didn't exactly rush to the polls and seize the day. Today the North-east feels like an under-funded province. There is a strong perception of Central Belt-bias within the Scottish Parliament. Aberdeen has been told it will have to build its own bypass. The city council is refusing to.

Don't get me wrong. I'm chuffed to live in this peaceful, temperate part of the world, with its intoxicating scenery and stoical people, but I find Scotland exists only in a notional sense.

Scots do share similarities, but they share them with the world. The car ended the North-east's isolation and close-knit dependence; *The Archers* killed off bothy ballads and their equivalent in other parts the country; the internet is creating communities bound by common interest, not geography. Slowly the chary North-east character is disappearing. Kids in the Aberdeen readily anglicise their speech. They have learned universal phrases – and forgotten local ones. They dress like they're on MTV, in baseball caps and big-arsed jeans, as kids do in Kinlochleven and throughout Scotland.

We have become an amorphous whole, a jelly moulded by our ravaged coastline and the border with England.

But the new world is far from united. Differences define us. As people start to panic over the loss of identity they resurrect old enmities. In Britain you see this on the sports field. Whenever Scotland play England at football, for example, we become like one excitable, yappy dog.

# PAR 10,000

Scotland is a proud nation, yes, but an insecure one. Beneath the patriotic bluster there's a suspicion we might fail on our own; that we're simply not as good as the country across the border to which we're still tethered. In the North-east it is invariably new-comers who dominate local affairs, who run community groups and organise campaigns. We ourselves are slow to speak out, preferring action to words.

Sport is a chance to show what we're made of. Polticians may huff and puff about our comparative worth, but you can't argue with a scoreline. When Kenny Dalgish nut-megged Ray Clemence to win 2–1 in 1976, it was a piece of a wit to rival anything you will hear in Holyrood or Westminster. The match is our chance to bite the Auld Enemy on the bum.

I'm sure the game's cultural significance will wane as our political confidence grows. Walking across Scotland, I felt like I'd caught the country off-guard, with a girn on its face, as though it had been roused from slumber and was trying to find its bearings. Land access, farming policy, GM technology, rural poverty – these issues are now ours to wrestle with. There is a flickering of self-belief that might yet give rise to a singular voice.

It is December as I write, a month of short days and long shadows. There's a pervasive dampness in the North-east during the dark months, a cold, clammy sweat that spreads across pavements and rooftops, turning crispy leaves to slimy mulch. The land is sometimes held under a net of frost, and the wind is powerless to jangle plants. Even the sun seems lethargic, wounded by the cold as it struggles to climb above the spindly trees that look black and arthritic against the wan sky.

Not ideal weather for golf, then.

Snow, sleet, grainy light, mud stiff enough to scuff your clubs, squalls fierce enough to turn your umbrella into a cocktail decoration – it's a struggle at this time of year. But you will still see people out on the course, bent against the wind, digging the ground with their clubs – doing their best.

Some of the lowest scores are recorded at this time of year. That's because golf courses effectively contract during the cold months. 'Winter greens' are marked out towards the end of the fairway, away from bunkers which may be filled with iced water. On some courses players are required to tee-up on the fairway, making it easy to fly the ball with a driver. Frozen grass puts yet more yards on your shot. As the temperature drops, so does your score.

# SOLITAIRE IN A FIELD

Golf is like playing solitaire in a field. No other sport is so self-centred. Tiger Woods was berated for suggesting Ryder Cup players should be paid for taking part. Some inferred that he didn't see playing for his country as reward enough. Those who took umbrage misunderstood both Tiger and the game. Tiger Woods is assuredly proud to be American, but prouder still to be Tiger Woods.

I never thought I would have another sporting hero after Pelé and Ayrton Senna. In the evening after his first grand prix win in 1985, Senna could be found circling the Estoril track in a hire-car long after the other drivers had jetted home, looking for places he might have been quicker during the day. That is why I revere these guys: because they measure themselves against the clock or the par of a course, not against those around them. They are out there on their own.

Sure, Tiger was pleased to win the Open at St Andrews – the historic home of golf – in the millennial year. And yes, he said it felt wonderful to become the youngest player to complete the grand-slam of the Open, the US Open, the Professional Golfer's Association Championship and The Masters. But as he stood beside the 18th green in the chill of a Fife afternoon, this deity – his place among the sporting gods ordained by a series of almost Biblical contingencies – admitted that finishing a record 19 under par had been important too. That made his day complete.

Sometimes hitting a ball well isn't enough. Once you start keeping score (the curse of adulthood) it's very difficult to stop. It doesn't matter if you are playing the Old Course, a municipal 9, or crossing a mountain range with a club in your hand. Sport without scoring is like cooking without eating. Numbers provide context. They bring meaning to frivolity, order to madness. Par is but one tiny straightjacket around our terrifyingly arbitrary lives. And there was me thinking it might provide some incidental fun.

'Ah, but you took more than five minutes to look for a ball,' I can hear someone spluttering, and under Rule 27-a it should have been declared lost!

I won't pretend my score bears any great scrutiny. For a start the distances are approximations. There was no true rigour to the rules as I applied them whenever I found my ball sitting in cow shit or floating off down a burn – and I'm quite sure the Royal and Ancient wouldn't have offered an interpretation. According to Appendix I of the rulebook, they recommend that 'the Rules of Golf be observed uniformly'. However, this august body does concede:

# PAR 10,000

Adverse conditions are sometimes so general throughout a course that the [local] Committee believes preferred lies or winter rules would promote fair play or help protect the course. Heavy snows, spring thaws, prolonged rains or extreme heat can make fairways unsatisfactory and sometimes prevent use of heavy mowing equipment.

That's Scotland for you. And I'm not complaining.